EQUIP

EQUIP

a youth worker's guide to
developing student leaders

TIM MILBURN

bare
foot
MINISTRIES®

Copyright 2012 by Barefoot Ministries®

ISBN 978-0-8341-5062-1

Printed in the United States of America

Editor: Audra C. Marvin
Cover Design: Arthur Cherry
Interior Design: Sharon Page

Library of Congress Cataloging-in-Publication Data: 2011946125

10 9 8 7 6 5 4 3 2 1

DEDICATION

To Travis, Tori, Mitch, and Abby

ACKNOWLEDGMENTS

One of the central tenets of good leadership is the ability to get others involved. This is certainly true when one is writing a book on leadership development. I am fortunate to be surrounded by people who are a lot smarter than me. In many ways, everything I've written in this book is something I learned from someone else.

I want to thank Chris Folmsbee for giving me the opportunity and the one-day pep talk to get this book written. I appreciate the editing skills of Audra Marvin, who made sure all of the words are in the right order. I'm indebted to my league of extraordinary youth leaders, who gave me their thoughts and feedback: Kenny Wade, Nate Roskam, Brooklyn Lindsey, Keegan Lenker, James O'Connell, and Mike Kipp. You all do such a great job of raising up youth leaders who are invested in the process of raising up student leaders.

I am especially grateful to my students, both past and present, who are engaged in the process of leading. You make all of this so worthwhile with your passion to make a difference.

CONTENTS

INTRODUCTION

My first lesson in leadership happened in the third grade.

Our third grade class used a monitor system. Each monitor had certain tasks and responsibilities. At the beginning of the week, the teacher assigned different students in the class to be the monitors. Once selected, students served in those positions for the entire week.

Some monitor positions were more fun than others. For example, the flag monitor led everyone in the Pledge of Allegiance. The role monitor took attendance. The line monitor always stood at the front of the line, trying to get everyone into some semblance of a linear pattern.

But the most sought after of all positions was the eraser monitor. It was the king (or queen) of the monitors. When you were selected to be eraser monitor, you ruled the class.

While it required the most physical exertion of any of the monitors, it carried its own set of perks. First, it got you outside the classroom. Chalkboards were the norm in the classroom back then, and the process of removing the chalk from the erasers had to be performed outside. This gave the eraser monitor moments of freedom throughout the day. Second, it was just plain fun. The removal process involved banging erasers together. This created huge clouds of chalk dust through which one could run and get covered. You always came back into the classroom looking a bit pale.

It was the job every kid in my class wanted. It was the last job assigned each week. Our teacher seemed to understand the excitement and anticipation over who would be chosen for this role. When you were the eraser monitor, you had influence.

Whenever I think back to the first time I thought about leadership, I'm reminded of the role of eraser monitor. It is my earliest memory of being responsible for something. It's the first time I can recall being in a position that held some influence over others. It was my first step in what has become a lifelong journey around the lessons of leadership. And, like this first lesson, I've discovered that I've learned the most during those moments when I was involved in actually leading.

This carried on through high school and into college. I found my greatest fulfillment from leading. I was involved in student government and served in various roles at my youth group and church. At each stage, I learned how important leadership was for a group of people to accomplish meaningful endeavors, grow in significant ways, and become something together that they couldn't become on their own.

I started to read everything I could find on the subject of leadership. If a book or article had the word *leadership* in it, I was interested. I sought out wisdom and advice from others who appeared to lead well. Along the way, I found out that I not only had a love for learning about leadership; I was becoming more involved in teaching it to others. As a lifelong student of leadership, I committed to finding others who shared my passion.

I did the math the other day and was surprised by what I came up with. I've been developing student leaders for more than twenty-four years. I don't know if I should feel overwhelmed by that or just old. It's also surprising that it's taken me about a quarter of a century to put some of my own perspective and philosophy on developing student leaders into a book. While I've written a lot of articles, blog posts, and self-published manifestos on the subject, I'm grateful to the people who kept encouraging me to put what I've learned into a book.

Some students show better leadership potential than others. They display innate giftedness, charisma, or just a strong willingness to accept responsibility. But I don't want to limit leadership only to those who appear to have been born with the right skill set. There's something special about those students who aspire to be leaders. Having seen how difficult it can be, I want to do what I can to help them be successful. Leadership *can* be learned. Leadership principles can be applied by anyone, in any circumstance.

With this in mind, let me clear at the beginning: This isn't going to be a journey you'll walk with *every* student in your care. It's not that you *can't* offer leadership development to every student; it's more about using discernment to offer it to the students who really want it (and who will really use it).

Student leaders learn to lead *by* leading, just like we learn most everything else. You don't learn to ride a bike by watching a movie about riding a bike. You've got to get on the bike and pedal. It's in falling off that you learn the most about riding.

Most of the youth workers I come into contact with think leadership training is a good idea. They want to offer some form of it in their ministries. They understand the missional nature of the church and want to involve, rather than entertain, their students. The very nature of God's kingdom at work in the world around us demonstrates a clear need for strong leadership. Any significant endeavor is going to require someone, at some point, to be a leader.

We may know we need leaders. We may know that leadership can be developed. But we don't necessarily know how to start or what to do. So we think back to what leadership development looked like when we were students and end up with one of the following:

1) a program that was used on us when we were students in the youth ministry

2) a program borrowed from the academic or business arena

3) a program found in a leadership book or curriculum

If you're like me, I would pick up a book looking for the next great idea. *But I wasn't looking for another thing to do.* I understand that. I don't want to add another program to your plate. I don't believe programs are the best way to develop student leaders. But a process is.

You may not have time for the process. I realize you might have picked up this book simply looking for a way—a template, maybe—to develop student leaders. And while I've got some of my own ideas about what to do, I can't start there. I know because I've started there with a number of youth groups and come up short. I don't think we can begin to identify *what to do* until we think deeply about the *who* and *why*.

This book is more about the *who* and *why*. It doesn't offer a slick program with downloadable t-shirt designs and monthly meeting plans (although I always like a good t-shirt and think you should definitely have a plan). Rather, it starts with a personal look at *your* leadership development. Simply put: Developing leaders develop leaders. You need to reflect on your own leadership journey. Your best teaching moments will occur out of your own experiences and examples.

I also want you to think deeply about the type of student leader you seek to develop. What does the picture of an effective student leader look like in your youth ministry? Think about your efforts in the context of the church. There is a unique and significant contribution each of us can make in the advancement of God's kingdom. While there are some traditional components in leadership that are necessary in all situations, you're seeking to shape a different kind of leader. Developing leaders within the movement of *missio Dei* (mission of God) calls for

14
*

a different focus than developing students to serve on the sophomore class council or as officers of the Glee Club.

If your students are going to become leaders, you're going to have to let them actually lead. You may have to step back from something so your students can step up. This is going to be a process that requires some space. You and your student leaders are going to need some room to walk this journey together for a while. May God give you the wisdom and courage to create the space necessary.

SECTION ONE

THE YOUTH
~~WORKER~~ LEADER

LET'S TALK ABOUT YOU

If you're going to develop student leaders, the first person who needs to be developed is you. Too many leadership development programs are facilitated by people who have forgotten to start with themselves. I want you to get personal. I want you to spend some time thinking about how you will grow and mature in your own leadership skills. You got involved in youth ministry to walk alongside students. I want you to make sure you're equipped for the journey.

I know you probably picked up this book thinking it would lay out a plan—a neatly organized program designed to show you, step by step, how to develop leadership skills and abilities in your students. The good news is, we'll get to that. The better news is, we can't get to that until we spend some time talking about your leadership development. In a world of cut-and-paste programming, this book will probably let you down. That's not to say you won't create a program. I simply don't want you to start there.

Before we can talk about the process or the student, we have to spend some time talking about you. That may seem self-centered, but it's not. We see this illustrated every time we get on an airplane, do we not?

"Insert the tab into the metal fitting." Check.

"Locate the nearest exit." Check.

". . . seat cushion as a flotation device." Still a bit damp . . . Check.

"Secure the oxygen mask over your own nose and mouth. Then secure the mask over any small children." Che . . . Wait. What?

It's true, isn't it? Every time they give the demonstration, the instructions state you must put the air mask over your own nose and mouth before you assist anyone else, even that beloved child who can't breathe sitting next to you. Just doesn't seem right, does it?

Yet, there's wisdom in the process. If a child is struggling with his or her mask, you and I will be of no help if we pass out trying to assist them. We have to keep breathing so they can keep breathing.

The same is true in student leadership development. While it is not *about* the youth worker, it has to *start* with the youth worker. Your students are going to be watching you. They're observing you because they instinctively know that it starts with you. Like every person who submits to the leadership of another, they ask the question: *If you can't lead yourself, how can I trust you to lead me?*

WHO ARE YOU?

I don't know you, but I have some assumptions about who you might be. Ultimately, you are a youth worker I've dreamed up out of my own experience.

As I wrote each paragraph of this book I imagined you and I sitting across from each other at a table at my favorite Mexican restaurant, Chapala's. As we kept hammering through basket after basket of chips and salsa, I imagined us having a conversation about what it means to develop student leaders. I'll be honest; you always ate more chips than I did. But that's only because I was doing most of the talking.

While I saw you as an imaginary person, I know you are real, and you work with real students. If I were to describe you, I'd guess you have at least a few of the following characteristics:

You have been a student of leadership most of your life.

You want to prepare your students to be leaders.

You realize leadership development is closely linked to personal growth.

You have benefited from leadership development in your own life.

You're a volunteer, and the lead youth pastor handed you this book.

You believe leadership is biblical.

You don't like the leaders you currently have, and you want to raise up a new generation of leaders.

You know every single student will benefit from some form of leadership development.

You believe your church, your youth ministry, or your para-church ministry is the perfect place to invest in your students. And this is the perfect time.

You've seen the results of both good and bad leadership.

You want to teach students skills they can use in every area of their lives.

You want to provide your students with the tools to make a difference.

You want to raise up students who are recognized as leaders among their peers, in their schools, in their churches, and in their communities.

Am I close?

Each one of us has to figure out why we're doing this. I know you're busy and your plate is full (not just with chips and salsa). If you don't understand the *why* behind your investment, it will just become another thing you're doing. And if it's just another thing you're doing, you'll come up with all kinds of reasons to stop doing it.

This is why I don't want you to think about your students just yet. Let's just focus on you for a while.

YOUTH WORKER VS YOUTH LEADER

I know the subtitle of this book is "The Youth *Worker's* Guide . . ." But for our purposes here, we need to change your title. Up to this point, I've referred to you as a youth worker. I agreed to do so at the beginning of this book to please those who are paying for the paper and binding process. But going forward, I'm changing your name. If you are going to be involved in the process of developing student leaders, you need to be a leader yourself. A leader develops other leaders. So I hereby change your title to youth *leader*.

Now, just to be clear, I love youth workers. We need youth workers. But there's a very real difference between being a *worker* and being a *leader*. Both serve an important function, but they're not the same thing. And it's a lot more than semantics.

I define a youth worker as *someone who is mainly focused on accomplishing the necessary tasks associated with the youth ministry.* There's always a lot to do in youth ministry. You need someone to drive the van, get the supplies, organize the events, facilitate the activities, play the instruments, and so many other tasks. One person can't do it alone (although some of you may have tried). We will always need to recruit others to be involved and accomplish certain tasks within the youth ministry.

But a youth leader functions differently. I define a youth leader as *one who is mainly focused on the overall well-being and growth of the students and people associated with the youth ministry.*

To oversimplify it, a youth worker looks at the youth ministry and sees things to do; a youth leader looks at the youth ministry and sees people to nurture.

Some may ask, "Are you saying I'm not a youth leader because I have to do everything?"

Others are quick to tell me, "I'm the only one involved in our youth ministry. I am both youth worker and youth leader and whatever else you want to call it."

I'll do my best to explain the difference. Imagine you are hosting an all-nighter at your church. Both the youth worker and the youth leader will show up a little early and get everything ready to go. But they're looking at the event through different eyes. The youth worker will see all kinds of tasks that need to get done in order to have a successful lock-in. They'll need to prepare the food, run the games, keep students where they're supposed to be, and try to stay awake. The youth worker's approach is to do the tasks necessary to get through the event.

The youth leader sees it a bit differently. While a youth leader will be involved in doing all of the same tasks, the focus is different. Youth leaders see the all-nighter as an opportunity to build relationships. They are going to intentionally use these eight to ten hours to invest in their students' lives. They also recognize how this all-nighter fits into the bigger picture. It's not a stand-alone event, but rather it's part of an ongoing process to build community, foster relationships, and shape the lives of the students who are present.

One sees tasks; the other sees people.

Youth workers lead Bible studies and engage in conversations with students. But they see these responsibilities as tasks that need to be accomplished. You'll often hear them describe their work as something they need to get through. On the other side, youth leaders will mop floors and drive vans and whatever else needs to be done, yet they do it because they're working toward an outcome greater than simply completing the task—the nurture and growth of the students in their care.

Perhaps you find yourself somewhere in the middle. You see yourself as a youth wor-der or a youth lea-ker (you have no idea how much fun I had putting those words together). There might be some moments that you're all about the tasks and other moments when you see how truly the tasks are connected to accomplishing the mission of the youth ministry.

The truth is, no one can really know what your focus is except you. It's a matter of motive and perspective. It has a lot to do with those who do something in the youth ministry because it's the next thing to do and those who do something because they see the big picture and are working toward a certain outcome. But it's important to know whether, in general, you function as a youth worker or a youth leader. If we take the time to begin to think the way a leader thinks, then we'll start to do the things leaders do. Workers don't develop leaders. Workers accomplish tasks. Leaders develop other leaders.

It's important to make the worker-leader distinction right up front because, just as there's a difference between a youth worker and a youth leader, there's also a difference between a student worker and a student leader. Most of the leadership development programs I come across are really good at developing student workers but not necessarily student leaders. This often happens because we've placed youth workers in charge of our student leadership development.

Now, please don't go out and fire all of those good folks whom you identify as youth workers. Some people aren't able to invest a lot of time in the youth ministry but want to help in whatever ways they can. They'll show up to drive or bake cookies. They'll travel with us and assist on service projects and mission trips. They help us get done what needs to get done, and this is a good thing.

But I'll be honest and tell you that I deliberately go around trying to encourage every youth worker to become a youth leader. That's because I know students have a better shot at developing their leadership skills under the watchful eyes of leaders more so than workers. I also want adults to be engaged and immersed in the lives of our students, modeling their own faith journeys and moving our ministry toward a common vision. The good news is, you might already be there; you just haven't changed your title yet. We'll see.

THE LEADER'S LOGIC

If this whole student leadership endeavor is going to work, it has to start with the youth leader. As soon as youth leaders hear that, they're always interested to know how. *How do I become a better leader? How do I improve? What do I need to do?*

My answer isn't profound. It's a simple thing that requires a lot of time and practice. When you're engaged in it, it tends to look like you're not doing anything. I answer these types of questions by inviting youth leaders to spend more time *thinking*.

Victor Hugo stated, "A man is not idle because he is absorbed in thought. There is a visible labor and there is an invisible labor." I encourage youth leaders to invest more energy in this invisible labor. I know a lot of youth leaders who are busy with *doing* and not spending much time *thinking*. When that happens, one starts to move away from the role of youth leader.

I cut my teeth in youth ministry during a period of time that recognized youth workers as doers of good, at a moment's notice, by the seat of their pants. I might have been the poster child for spontaneity. I survived many Sunday mornings, teaching times, and last-minute projects because of my ability to produce *on the fly*. While some may see this as a strength, it can quickly become a liability. It will also tear away at the credibility of one's leadership because you find yourself only doing what's urgent, with a limited knowledge of what's important with a well-thought-out plan. The way you confront and overcome this tendency is to spend more time thinking.

So the leader's logic is this: *In order to do the things a leader does, you need to think the way a leader thinks.* The leader's logic is an important principle. It has helped me in my own growth as a leader. It guides me through difficult decisions and inspires me to look at situations from different perspectives. Thinking is hard work. Sometimes we just want to dive in and get going. Yet the very things that separate youth workers from youth leaders are the time they spend thinking and what they think about.

I've seen the leader's logic played out on many of the service projects and mission trips I've led. Without fail, there is always something that doesn't go as planned. I've had van breakdowns, flat tires, sick students, failed projects, unavailable supplies, and so many other unexpected incidents. Leaders are problem solvers. If a leader doesn't take the time to think through a problem, he or she runs the risk of reacting to it in a way that may not produce the best outcome.

On one trip, I led a group of students and adult volunteers to serve a church in a low-income community in southern Arizona. Our work focused on construction, painting, and minor maintenance. We arrived at the church late in the evening. The pastor and his family were there to greet us and help us get settled in our sleeping arrangements on the floor of the church.

We got up early the next morning to get started before the Arizona heat overwhelmed us. While we ate breakfast with the pastor and a couple of wonderful ladies from the church who helped prepare our meal, we asked where the pre-arranged supplies had been delivered. Before leaving town, we called and purchased many of our materials from a local building and supply company so we wouldn't have to haul everything ourselves. The pastor looked confused. I distinctly remember him looking at us and saying, "Materials? What materials? We thought you'd be bringing all of your supplies with you."

We all looked at each other in stunned silence. One of our construction foremen quickly got up to make some calls. I began to think about what we were going to do for the next five days. A few minutes later, our foreman came back with a forlorn look on his face. The building and supply company thought we were coming in the next week. They could get us what we needed, but it would take three days. He told us there would be no way to complete the project we had come to do in the amount of time we would have left.

I pulled our group of adults together along with the pastor and started to think through our options. A couple of them felt like we should head home and come back at a later date. Others were willing to stay a couple of extra days and complete the project without the students. Most of the adults felt like we couldn't keep the students there with nothing to do. The pastor just sat there and listened.

Someone looked over at me and asked, "So what are we going to do?" In that moment, I felt the full weight of leading this group. I wanted to come up with some way to save the project. I also knew what our students had gone through to get there. Many had saved and put effort into fundraisers. We couldn't just turn around and go home.

I stared at the table for a moment and then simply said, "I need to think about it for a little bit." Everyone seemed okay with that. "I'm going for a walk," I told the group. Over the next forty-five minutes I did a lot of thinking and praying. I felt responsible. I didn't know what to do. Then, somewhere between the edge of the church property and an alley leading down the street, I had an idea.

My thought process leading up to the idea went something like this: *We're stuck. This is going to fail. Our students worked so hard to be here. Our students needed to help these people. These people are going to be disappointed in us. These people needed us to build something for them. These people need our students. Our students need these people.* BAM! Once the idea hit me, I got really excited. It may not appear earth shattering to you, but this idea set the stage for one of the best trips I've taken students on. My idea was this: *We are going to build relationships between our church and their church, doing whatever it takes.*

As I look back on that trip, I remember how we decided to gather in services with their church every day. We put on a low-key, low-budget Vacation Bible School for the kids. We got enough supplies to do some of the maintenance work and a little of the painting. We ate every meal with different people from the church. We put on an event for them to invite their neighbors to come and enjoy. As we pulled away from the church to return home, we discovered we had made a lot of great friendships and created some wonderful memories.

I'm not saying my idea that saved the day. What I *will* say is that I learned that thinking through the situation rather than reacting to it helped me identify what the trip was really all about. It wasn't about building a structure. It was about building relationships. And when I explained that to the group, everyone agreed. Then we put everything we had into doing just that.

INSPIRATION AND EVALUATION

Most people have the capacity to learn and grow in their leadership skills. Even if you don't think you're a good leader, you can get better at leadership. Part of your growth will happen as a result of your thinking. This is why it's crucial to become more intentional in your thinking as a leader.

When I invite people to spend more time thinking, they initially wonder, *What do I think about?* All they can picture is sitting in an open field, daydreaming about life and allowing any and every thought to carry them where it will. That's not what I mean by thinking. To put it simply, thinking precedes leading. In fact, leading that isn't preceded by thinking is called reacting.

When was the last time you thought deeply about your own leadership development? The truth is, there's a lot to think about. I recommend focusing on two different types of thinking: inspiration and evaluation.

Inspiration thinking is the ability to look at a situation and figure out what will move a group of people one step closer toward accomplishing their mission. It looks forward. It keeps the vision clear and compelling in the minds of people. It recognizes the unique contribution each individual can make and encourages its use for the good of the group.

Evaluation thinking stops to consider what has taken place and figure out what worked and what didn't. It seeks to commend the efforts that go well and correct the efforts that don't. It is always on the lookout for lessons learned. It makes the most of every situation, learning from mistakes and improving on successes. It looks back with an eye toward continual growth.

This is the type of thinking Jesus encourages his followers to engage in as they wrestle with the cost of discipleship:

> Suppose one of you wants to build a tower. Won't you first sit down and estimate the cost to see if you have enough money to complete it? For if you lay the foundation and are not able to finish it, everyone who sees it will ridicule you, saying, "This person began to build and wasn't able to finish." Or suppose a king is about to go to war against another king. Won't he first sit down and consider whether he is able with ten thousand men to oppose the one coming against him with twenty thousand? If he is not able, he will send a delegation while the other is still a long way off and will ask for terms of peace.
>
> Luke 14:28-32, TNIV

Inspiration thinking looks forward and asks the question: *Can I?* Evaluation thinking looks back and asks the question: *Will I?* Both are important in the consideration of any endeavor.

THE SIX *P*s

Armed with these two types of thinking, I want to provide you with six key areas that help set the tone for your own leadership development. I call these The Six *P*s. They are:

1 Perspective

2 Passion

3 Position

4 Persistence

5 Personal Philosophy

6 Priorities

Remember, what you do as a leader will flow out of your thinking in each of these areas.

But wait, there's one more. In fact, it is the most crucial and is the overarching practice I would add as an addendum to each item on this list. Prayer.

Prayer isn't the same thing as thinking. We probably use some of the same brain muscles, but there is a difference. Thinking is a conversation you have with yourself. Prayer is a conversation you have with God. Prayer should not be an afterthought in this process. My prayers sometimes *feel* like my own thoughts. And most of the time, my thoughts flow out of prayerful yearnings. Sometimes it's hard to tell the difference between prayerful thoughts and thoughtful prayers. Looking back at my thought process with the group in southern Arizona, most of my thoughts started with the question, *God, what should we do?*

Think of prayer as the umbrella that rests over these other six components. It's a way to interact and reflect on each one. God is intimately interested in how you grow and develop in your leadership. Prayer separates self-guided leaders from Spirit-led leaders. A prayerful and thoughtful approach through each of these areas will have a direct impact on the type of leader you become.

29
*

PERSPECTIVE IS YOUR LEADERSHIP LENS

It's important that you develop and claim a definition of leadership. My own leadership perspective has been shaped by a variety of definitions. Someone sees leadership in action and makes an observation. Over time, those observations are proven true in a variety of experiences. These are then offered as defining statements that shed light on what leadership looks like.

The conglomeration of leadership descriptions I have embraced and molded into my definition involves a focus on followers, an emphasis on vision, and a recognition that leadership is not coercive. These ideas validate the tenets of leadership I think are most important, but they don't identify all there is to know about leadership. They identify my perspective.

In the process of identifying *your* perspective, you'll begin to notice that the way you see leadership is different from the way others see it. You'll refer back to the leaders in your life, both good and bad. Your perspective will be shaped by the stories and experiences that shaped you. We can learn to appreciate the differences that exist from the variety of perspectives we encounter.

Your perspective is the lens through which you'll view the day-to-day life of your youth ministry. This lens, shaped by your past, is placed before you as a way to view your future. Before you picked up this book, you might never have looked at the leadership potential or opportunities in your youth ministry. Now, as you read through it and begin to invest in thinking and praying about your leadership and your ministry, these words will begin to affect your lens.

We tend to see what we're looking for. It's the way God has wired us. For example, I drive a white pickup truck, and now I see all the other white pickup trucks of the same make and model on the road.

30
*

Owning a white pickup changed my perspective. It changed what I was looking for.

It will be difficult to see the opportunities to develop student leaders if you're not looking for them. As you take the time to think and pray about your leadership, you'll nurture your leadership perspective. You'll grow in your ability to point out the leadership lessons that occur all around us. You'll see things that others might miss simply because they weren't looking for them. As you develop your leadership lens, you'll be better prepared to teach students how to develop that type of perspective in their own lives.

Let me describe what this looks like. Our campus selects students to help us build relationships with the community that surrounds us. One day, Ben, a student selected to serve in this capacity, asked for my help for a local blood drive he was hosting. While I oversee Ben and his community relations office, this is his event. He is leading it. He approached me the day before the blood drive and told me he needed help moving some chairs. I agreed to help him. I'm always happy to help. But Ben hadn't been completely forthright, and two things became quickly apparent. "Some" chairs actually meant a whole lot of chairs, and "moving" meant hauling by truck and up multiple flights of stairs. This was a much bigger job than just "moving some chairs."

As we huffed and puffed up a flight of stairs, each lugging chairs in both hands, I asked Ben where all his volunteers were. (I was feeling it at this point, and I honestly hoped more people might join in. But that's not the reason I asked the question. This question wasn't about moving chairs.) I wanted to know if he saw the situation like I saw the situation. I wanted to know what his leadership perspective was. Beyond the simple (or not so simple) task of moving chairs, I was wondering about his *investment* in people through all the tasks it took to conduct a blood drive. I wanted to know if he too was wondering where all his volunteers were.

This moment became a teachable moment about his perspective on leadership, especially as it related to pulling off this blood drive. It only happened because I was already viewing the situation from a leadership perspective. Getting a group of people to move chairs instead of doing it all by yourself (or asking your advisor) was a step in the right direction, but it wasn't the real issue. If all you see are the tasks, then you're functioning in the role of youth worker.

The youth *worker* is going to enter into this situation and look at Ben and say something like, "Many hands make light work." This is a great platitude for someone who is focused on getting the task done. But my perspective wanted to draw something a little different and a little deeper from the situation. It wasn't a question about *getting* more people so much as it was an opportunity to talk about *investing* in more people. I wanted to make sure Ben was thinking like a leader thinks.

THE PUSH OF PASSION

Do you know what you're passionate about? I realize the term *passion* can get a little confusing. It can run the gamut from a strong emotion to a vice of human nature to a life calling. Despite the various connotations (kind of like the word *love*), I think it's a great word. I'm using it here to recognize and describe who you are.

I intentionally decided to use the word passion instead of purpose (do you realize how many great words there are that start with the letter *p*?). Your life's purpose is like a compass that gives you direction in life. But passion is the energy that moves you forward in that direction. It is the willingness to do something you love *because* you love doing it. You would do it, and do it well, even if you weren't getting paid for it (welcome to youth ministry). One of my favorite descriptions of passion is: Find something you love to do so much that you'd gladly do it for nothing. Then learn to do it so well that people are happy to pay you for it.

I don't think any book on leadership would be complete without an Oprah quote. I thought I'd get mine out of the way early but only because it's so fitting here. As Oprah faced the camera on May 25, 2011, in her last episode of *The Oprah Winfrey Show*, having run nationally since September 8, 1986, for 25 seasons and 4,561 episodes, she had this to say about the experience: "That's what passion is; it's a calling. It lights you up and lets you know that you are exactly where you are supposed to be, doing exactly what you are supposed to be doing."

I would guess there aren't too many of us out there who can do what Oprah did, and for that long. But one thing we all have in common with Oprah is that we each carry a passion. Maybe you already know what yours is. Maybe you still need to discover it. Here's one way to find out. Think about what keeps you up at night and what gets you up early in the morning. And no, the answer isn't worry.

You're passionate about the things you care the most about. You care most about the things you're passionate about. That may be one of the very reasons you signed on to be a youth leader. You care deeply for the young people in your faith community.

There's a push-pull dynamic in place when it comes to leadership roles. Most people are pulled into leadership because of the permission of others. They go through some type of selection process that's based on the positive recommendations of other people. On the other side, there's something that pushes us toward certain opportunities and roles: passion! Passion is the internal motivation and energy. When you feel that push to step up and lead, it's likely that your passion is doing some of the pushing. In fact, when others consider giving you permis-

33
*

sion to lead in a certain area, they are trying to see if it's something you're passionate about.

When it comes to leadership development, take the time to identify where your passions lie. Your passions will influence your motives, expectations, dreams, and desires. The path to leadership for your students doesn't have to start in the form of a position. It can begin by helping them identify their God-given passions. When they begin to serve in the areas they care most about, it will push them toward opportunities to lead in those areas. The best leaders in my ministries first got involved because they were so passionate about the cause.

Any effort to develop students who are passionate to follow Christ and lead his church will be superficial if that passion doesn't exist within us. I encourage you to pray for the passion to develop student leaders. Students won't remember every lesson and every conversation. But they will remember when you took the flame that burned brightly inside you and used it to ignite the flame within them.

POSITION IS A PLATFORM

Every person holds a position of influence. Some are just more formal than others.

When it comes to leadership development, especially among our students, we must begin where we are. In our culture it's obvious that most people recognize leadership through the perspective of position. We like titles. Some titles are synonymous with leadership: president, director, king, boss, pastor, etc. In many ways, a position is an honorable means to exert influence over others. Position is the permission side of leadership. Most people assume positions because they are placed there by others.

But having a position of leadership doesn't mean one *is* a leader.

Think about your position. Why are you a youth worker, soon to be youth leader? Your position is a platform to exert a certain kind of influence in the lives of your students. You get to make some choices about how you will handle this position. You get to breathe life into this position with the uniqueness that only you can bring. A position doesn't define you but serves as means to express your God-given gifts and abilities for the good of others. Simply having a position—like having a title—doesn't make you a leader.

How are you glorifying God through your position? Your position gives you access to the lives of others that you didn't have before. It's an opportunity. When students show up to a youth group meeting or event, when you are riding or driving to your next activity, when students see your life and involvement—all of these opportunities are provided because you hold a unique position. Your position in the youth ministry is a launch pad to connect and guide. Position alone doesn't mean you're a leader. It's what you do while you hold the position that will define your leadership.

A position may give you initial credibility, but it's not a lasting credibility until you actually do something meaningful. Students will be watching you. They'll not only be observing how you lead them; they'll be evaluating how well you lead yourself, and that's exactly what you're hoping for. The example you provide will be your most powerful illustration of leadership.

PERSISTENCE PROVIDES CONTEXT

How long are you going to stick with this? This is an important question to ask at the beginning of the student leadership development process. Are you in it for a season or a couple of sessions? Persistence is the ability to maintain action regardless of your feelings. You press on even when you feel like quitting.

The good news is that this isn't a book about demonstrating or promoting another program for you to implement in your youth ministry. When it comes to developing leaders, I'm not interested in promoting a program because programs typically have a beginning and an end (unless they involve the words *Sunday* and *school*).

I am going to describe a process. This process looks less like showing up for a class and more like training for a marathon. It walks with a student through the highs and lows of leading. It's not about taking the next six weeks to talk about leadership, although I don't think that would hurt. This is going to be more than a one-month chapter in your curriculum. The timeline will be fuzzy. The requirements will vary. This will probably end up being more demanding than you initially thought, but it will be more rewarding as well.

Before you invite students to commit to develop their leadership skills, you will need to commit to developing your own leadership. Then you'll need to commit to being a part of the process of developing leadership within your students. There's a lot of commitment to consider. It's easy to make commitments; it's much harder to manage the commitments you make. It is your persistence in this process that adds value. This is not a process you have to engage in for the rest of your life, but it *is* a process you should engage in for the rest of your students' lives in your youth ministry. That may be too long for some. In my experience, it often wasn't long enough.

In order for leadership development to take root, it must become part of the culture of your youth ministry. Even saying it needs to be a "part" doesn't sound strong enough to me. That makes it seem like it can stand alone. A better way to picture this process is to say that it needs to be woven into the culture of your youth ministry. When that happens, it has the potential to change the way you function as a youth ministry. And in order for it to take hold within your culture, it's going to need staying power. That means the people with the leadership perspective and passion need to stay put for a while.

Persistence leads to longevity. Longevity breeds maturity. Longevity and maturity together will give those involved greater influence as they discover what works well and what doesn't. They will provide context for other areas of your youth ministry. They will shape the way you involve, train, and release people to serve and lead. People will recognize that students who walk through your ministry come out as better prepared leaders.

Persistence is especially important in the early stages of creating a leadership development culture. You will meet your greatest resistance in the early stages of the process. It will come from parents, other church leaders, even students who may not understand or feel like this is what they want to be a part of. How will you respond if students don't initially see the value, benefit, or need to develop their leadership abilities? You may even find that *you're* distracted by the next book you pick up or youth ministry workshop that challenges you to incorporate its ideas into your youth ministry. Even with the best intentions and commitment, your first, second, or even third attempts at developing student leaders may fail. What then?

I assure you, I'm not asking you to keep going *no matter what*. There's no honor in clinging to a process that no longer inspires you or the students in your care.

I recently tried to help a youth leader know when it was truly time to step away from something that just wasn't working. I told him, "Persistence is not stubbornness."

His response was, "It kind of depends, doesn't it?"

I said, "Absolutely. Persistence is willing to be open to *it depends*. Stubbornness is defiantly closed."

Unlike some commitments, I don't think you need to be in this thing until death do you part. But it will require more stamina than a junior high lock-in on back-to-back nights. I'm asking you to stick with this for the long haul because there is a great need for our youth ministries to develop student leaders. We are called to invest in the next generation who will lead the church. The group of people who are best prepared to do this is the church itself.

This is a stewardship issue. It is clear that it's God's church. But I haven't received the memo that tells me God has stopped using people to lead and guide his church. So until that message comes, I want to be someone who prayerfully and thoughtfully equips the youth for those moments when they have the opportunity to lead (and, in my mind, that's sooner rather than later).

YOUR PHILOSOPHY IS PERSONAL

How does student leadership development fit into your overall philosophy of youth ministry? Your philosophy of leadership is closely tied to your perspective on leadership because it shapes how you view it. But your philosophy also evolves from the opinions, priorities, and experiences you've had. For example, you might value leadership development in the context of youth ministry because that's what you experienced as a student. Or someone you respect in youth ministry has developed a culture that values leadership.

Not only do you have a philosophy of leadership, but you have a philosophy about church, the Bible, even God. Basically, your philosophy is constantly working to answer the question: *What am I supposed to be doing?*

I remember one of the first times I was forced to confront my own philosophy in youth ministry. It started around a conversation I was having with some of the other youth leaders in our group. We were discussing the upcoming road trip, and one of them asked me what kind of music I was going to allow the students to listen to in the van. The question and my answer (Christian music!) seemed simple enough. Yet I got a little pushback from a couple of the other leaders: Why?

In my experience, we listened to Christian music on the van ride to events because we were a Christian group traveling to a Christian event in what we considered to be a Christian van (it had the name of our church on the side). That's as far as I had gone with it. That was the heart of my why. So that's what I told them.

My youth leaders weren't content. *How do you define Christian music? Isn't there other music that honors God but doesn't mention his name? What about music by non-Christians that appears to support Christian principles?*

I wasn't prepared to answer their questions. I hadn't developed or determined my philosophy of music on road trips beyond the level of *we do what we've always done.* I'm not going to tell you how this whole thing turned out or what we came up with. Every group is different, and if you're simply copying someone else's philosophy, you probably haven't done the hard work to really make it your own.

At this point, let's step back from the discussion about music and consider your philosophy of student leadership. Since we all operate with various perspectives and philosophies, it's important to identify what yours is. Your philosophy influences what you spend your time on and what you don't. At some point in this process, someone connected to your youth ministry will approach you, wanting to have a conversation about the philosophy at work within the youth ministry and how it doesn't line up with theirs. If you haven't taken the time to prayerfully and thoughtfully work to identify your philosophy, it's going to be an even more difficult conversation.

I discovered early on that you cannot function well in youth ministry if you're constantly trying to appease the personal philosophies of everyone else. In the end, you please no one. It's best to make sure that your philosophy lines up well with the leadership of your church, ministry, or organization. Your philosophy should support the values and the mission of your local congregation and the community you serve. If it doesn't, then it's time to change your philosophy or change locations.

I can't caution you enough here. If you begin to incorporate and grow a strong student leadership culture in your youth ministry and it doesn't line up with your organization's philosophy, conflict on some level is right around the corner. Even if everyone is on board with the value of leadership development, it will still be necessary to discuss and define your approach. Your philosophy will answer questions about levels of responsibility given to students, accountability, and the type of opportunities you will allow students to lead.

Finally, it's not enough merely to *have* a philosophy. You must also be able to *articulate* your philosophy—to explain it in the face of competing philosophies. You won't be able to move forward until the leaders under whom you serve offer their belief in your philosophy from the beginning. Don't surprise them with this kind of change. When it comes to change, nobody really likes surprises. (You can consider that free leadership advice.)

PRACTICAL DAILY PRIORITIES

The last *P* is a little different from the first five. You can count off the first five on one hand. As you raise your other hand to signify the sixth one, you'll see that it stands alone. The first five shape who you are and who you are becoming. They force you to reflect on what you believe. Each one will directly impact how you view both your role in and relationship to the youth ministry. The first five *P*s are the soil from which your leadership will grow. The sixth area—priorities—addresses how you'll work the land.

You can't do everything. Those who try to do everything typically end up doing nothing well. At some point, you have to look at the options available and figure out what's crucial. You and I make decisions every day, prioritizing one task or activity over another. We may spend a great deal of time thinking and praying about our passions and position, but until they show up in the activities of our day, they're just good ideas. The way we get good ideas out of our head is by acting on them. Prioritizing disciplines you to act on the right ideas.

Prioritizing protects you from spending the majority of your day dealing with the next urgent demand. It not only separates the important from the urgent; it identifies what is most crucial. Living each day with clearly formed priorities helps you know what to say yes to and what you'll say no to as well. William James said that wisdom is merely the art of knowing what to overlook.

Do you know what your priorities are? If you don't, I could probably figure them out for you. I have a unique ability to be able to tell what's important in someone's life—to peek behind the curtain and see what a person's real priorities are. Actually, the ability isn't all that unique, and you have it as well. All you have to do is observe what and how you spend on a daily basis in the following areas:

A. Your calendar; how you spend your time.

B. Your budget; how you spend your money.

C. Your commitments; how you spend your energy.

We all have priorities, even if we don't know them or haven't identified them. Sometimes we confuse ourselves by listing our ideal priorities but living out our actual priorities. Ideal priorities are areas we think are important and hope or wish to spend more time on. But at the end of the day, our lives don't reflect that list. If we're honest, we

41
*

often discover that our ideal priorities don't line up with our actual priorities. Actual priorities are what anyone could observe you actually doing on a regular basis.

Living with this type of disconnect is like shooting an arrow at the side of a barn and then walking up and drawing the target around it. Listing your priorities is not the same thing as living your priorities. A better question to ask might be: *Are my priorities in line with my perspective, my passion, my position, my persistence, and my philosophy—and am I living those out?*

Leadership development, both for you and your students, needs to become a priority. If it's important, it needs to show up regularly on your calendar and in your commitments. It's too important to let it happen by chance. Youth leaders make leadership development a priority.

Take a minute right now and write down everything you do in the youth ministry. As you look over your list, you'll need to make some decisions. Mark the very important items with an *A*. Now mark the somewhat important items with a *B*. The rest of the items are considered not important, and you can place a *C* next to them.

Now look at your list. My hope is that somewhere you listed *develop student leaders* and put an *A* next to it. I understand if you don't see it as a priority right now. You might not realize how important it is at this point (which is why I'm glad you have this book). I also understand if we part ways on this point. You might not be willing to invest in this area on a regular basis. That's okay. You have to make that decision just like everyone else. I do think it's helpful to identify where it fits on your list of priorities. I've seen it listed as an *A*, a *B*, and a *C*, and what I've found is that the lower it goes, the less effective it will be.

Leadership development, done well, enhances and grows all the other areas of youth ministry. Even ministries that are too big to fail will slowly grow emaciated and weak in the face of poor leadership. It is poor stewardship not to invest in and develop the next generation of leaders within the church. The adults who oversee our youth ministries must become better leaders not only for the present moment but also to serve as an example to those who will follow in their footsteps.

Think about your own church, ministry, or organization for a moment. How did God use effective leadership to advance the ministry? What happened in the face of poor leadership? Isn't the prayer of every ministry and movement that God would raise up strong leaders to carry on?

If you're serious about leadership development in the context of your youth ministry, then you'll make it a priority. And it's not difficult to tell whether its priority level is *A*, *B*, or *C*. Simply ask yourself these questions:

Did you spend any time on it?

Did you spend any money (resources) on it?

Did you spend any energy on it?

LEARNING LEADERSHIP FROM YOU

Jonathan came into my office and wanted to chat. As he sat there looking across the room at me, he started to smile.

"What's with the goofy grin, Jonathan?" I asked.

He looked me square in the eye and said, "I think I want to do what you're doing. How much longer are you going to stick around?"

I started to smile as well. "Are you saying you're going to take my job?"

Jonathan laughed. Then he said something I'll never forget. "No way. I don't want your job. I just want to keep watching you do your job so I'll know what to do when my time comes."

And all I could think at that moment was, *No pressure.*

43
*

Your students are going to learn how to lead by observing how you lead, both yourself and others. That may seem scary. No one knows you better than you. It's going to be two parts humbling and one part intimidating. Over time, it's who you are on the inside that's going to show through in what you do on the outside. The best leaders are developed from the inside out.

It's a lot easier to teach about leadership than it is to actually lead something. Moving from youth worker to youth leader is more than a change in title. It's a change in responsibility. You accept the responsibility to develop student leaders because that's what leaders do—raise up other leaders. Your example becomes the primary illustration students will use to think about their own examples.

People do what people see. Your students are more likely to lead the right way once they've seen you lead the right way. At the very least, they'll have an idea of what it looks like. You set the example by developing your own leadership skills. You set the example by being transparent about your own leadership journey. You set the example by sharing how to think like a leader thinks.

Leadership development is more than knowing how to execute the right skills. It flows out of the type of person you are. Leaders influence others based on who they are as well as what they do (and what they ask others to do). That's what makes leadership development different from, say, learning how to fix a car or conjugate a verb. If all it required was learning a certain skill set, more people would step into leadership. It's different because who you are on the inside will have a direct bearing on your capacity and credibility as a leader.

There are a variety of ways to teach leadership. You can teach from a book, from a video, from a curriculum. But the lessons your students will remember more than any others are the ones they experience. They will learn to lead themselves by watching you lead yourself. They will learn to lead others by watching the way you lead them. Then they will learn to lead through the act of leading. The whole process starts with you—the youth leader.

I like to illustrate the power of example with an imaginative exercise. I'm going to name a place, and I want you to tell me the first thing that pops into your mind. Ready?

Paris, France.

It's unfortunate that I can't hear your response. But if you're like the majority of the people I've done this exercise with, the first thought in your mind was an image of the Eiffel Tower.

There's a reason that most, if not all, of us think of the Eiffel Tower when we first hear the words *Paris, France*. It's because we think in images and pictures before we think in data or facts. I've never had anyone tell me their first thought was the population count or gross national product or even Paris's current fashion trends. They all thought of the Eiffel Tower because that monument is the picture of Paris, France, in most people's minds.

The same principle is at work when you set the example as a leader. Your example, lived out in front of the students you're leading and teaching, can become the image—the picture in their minds—they refer to when they think about leadership.

You can become the picture in your students' minds even if you're not in a formal position of leadership. You don't need a title. You don't need to be in a role where you're always up front. Leadership can come in many forms and from anywhere. Every person has the potential to influence others from right where they're at. Leadership is available to everyone in some form. What separates leaders from the rest is their willingness to take responsibility when an opportunity presents itself.

The following is a list of ways I've seen people step into leadership without ever having a title or formal position. You set the example when you:

- see a need and meet it.
- have an idea and implement it.
- create an activity and organize it.
- come up with a plan and unleash it.
- take a project and run with it.
- set a team goal and rally others around it.
- gather a team and take charge of it.
- encounter a problem and take care of it.
- implement a vision and work toward it.

Each of these actions is necessary in youth ministry. This is what youth leaders do. They take responsibility and then take others with them. They're willing to lead, often without being asked or assigned a formal role.

Every time you lead something or someone, it's an opportunity to model what effective leadership looks like. It's your example that people remember. It becomes the picture in people's minds that adds credibility to any lesson you might teach students about leadership. When you lead from the inside out, your example not only shows *what* you do but also gives you an opportunity to explain *how* and *why* you do it.

THE RIGHT KIND OF EXAMPLE

I always knew how important the idea of setting the example was to leadership. Time and again I heard great leaders talking about why they went first or how their service inspired others to serve. But the thing that makes the power of example foundational to developing student leaders is the fact that it is a biblical principle.

The Gospel of John records one of Jesus's most humbling acts. It's during the final days leading up to his crucifixion and ultimate resurrection. He is gathered in a room with his disciples to celebrate the Passover meal. They're getting situated and realize there isn't anyone there—a servant—to offer the traditional foot washing. I can imagine them all looking around the room, wondering who is in charge of this small but significant detail. No one in the room steps up to wash the feet of their friends and fellow disciples. Each is probably looking around to gauge which of them holds the lowest standing in the group because the foot washer is not only a servant in a dirty-job sense but also in the sense of a lower societal and cultural position.

The twist occurs when Jesus gets up and begins to disrobe. Stunned silence and growing shame probably fill the room as Jesus wraps a towel around his waist, grabs the cleaning supplies, and goes to work on the feet of his followers.

The leadership lesson is profound and immediate. For those who missed it in the group, Jesus explains what has just happened: "Now that I, your Lord and Teacher, have washed your feet, you also should wash one another's feet. I have *set you an example* that you should do as I have done for you" (John 13:14-15, emphasis added).

47
✳

Jesus doesn't teach the lesson with handouts and a nifty Power-Point presentation. He doesn't discuss the benefits of foot washing by titled leaders of a small, upstart rebellion. It appears he doesn't even use words until he is questioned by Peter during the lesson. The power of the lesson is in its display. Jesus creates the picture in his disciples' minds—an image they won't soon forget.

There's another place in Scripture where this is demonstrated in a way that may relate more to your role as a youth leader. The apostle Paul is heavily engaged in his own form of student leadership development when he writes his first letter of instruction to young Timothy.

Timothy might be in his late twenties or early thirties, but he still faces a leadership crisis tied to his youth. He has been placed in charge of the newly planted church in Ephesus. Paul and Timothy have a type of father-son relationship. Paul is Timothy's mentor. Timothy learns his leadership lessons from Paul.

As we read Paul's first letter to his protégé, it appears Timothy is having difficulty establishing a sense of credibility in his leadership role, especially with the older folks. It is in response to this that Paul offers the following advice: "Don't let anyone look down on you because you are young, but *set an example* for the believers in speech, in conduct, in love, in faith, and in purity" (1 Timothy 4:12, emphasis added).

Think about what Paul could say. He could tell Timothy to preach better sermons. He could instruct to him to throw Paul's name around a little. He might tell him he is going to come and set the people straight. But Paul doesn't offer Timothy anything that sounds even remotely close to that. The basis of his leadership wisdom hinges on three words: *Set an example.* Timothy can develop his leadership, gain credibility and influence, and silence his opposition all through the way he lives his life in front of those in his care.

Paul doesn't ask Timothy to simply follow one of the many examples people can recall; he advises him to *set* an example. He wants Timothy to become the picture in people's minds when it comes to the manner in which one lives out the life of faith. Timothy's influence won't come from motivational speeches or titles of authority. His leadership will arise from the way he lives his life in front of those around him. He will live in such a way that others will not only take notice but will seek to emulate the way he lives.

There's a difference between being an example and setting an example. Everyone can be an example. Whenever someone observes the manner in which we live, we are being examples of some kind. As

48
*

regular people, we hope we are being a good example. We hope we live and behave in such a way that others think well of us. But as leaders, we must strive to set an example. We must go first. We must show others how. We must live lives that raise the bar that others reach toward.

This is why it can be so devastating when a leader falls. People look to leadership to create the picture of how we're all going to move forward. When a leader falls because of a moral failure or a lack of character or breaking the law, people feel lost because they have to find a new example.

Setting the example can be done right where you're at. The disciples of Jesus don't have any formal titles. Timothy is considered by some to be too young to be in leadership. There aren't any prerequisites to setting the example, except to know and understand what kind of example you are trying to set. Paul expects Timothy to know the difference between the right way (God's way) and the wrong way to speak, conduct himself, love, exhibit faith, and live in purity. Timothy's influence will grow as he lives these out in front of the believers, especially the old folks.

As a youth leader, you already know you don't have any control over what your students think. You can't do anything to make your students feel a certain way about your leadership. You only have control of yourself. The process of thinking and praying through the Six *P*s helps us know we're doing the right things for the right reasons. We want to set the right kind of example.

Paul is helping Timothy understand that the first person a leader must lead is him or herself. It has to start with Timothy. He can preach a sermon series on Christian conduct. He can set up a midweek Bible study that works through all the passages dealing with faith. He can teach on these subjects over and over. Yet his greatest influence will

49
✳

come as he simply lives each of these areas out in front of his people in a way they can see it and repeat it in their own lives.

We all follow someone's example. Paul doesn't instruct Timothy to *be* an example but to *set* an example. It might sound similar, but there's a difference. He is encouraging Timothy to live his life in such a way that it will be emulated by others. Think about this in terms of leadership development. How many times have you been in a situation and wondered how a certain person might handle it?

This was the principle at work throughout the whole *WWJD?* craze. Drawing from the book *In His Steps*, by Charles Sheldon, people began to ask the question every time they were in a situation where they felt like they needed divine guidance. I can recall a moment where this movement made its mark on my family, although not in a way I would have expected.

When my kids were younger, there was a game we played every time we were getting in the car to go somewhere. There was always a battle to see who would sit in the front seat. (I'm sure anyone who has had children is familiar with this game. In fact, you've probably played it yourself.) In our family, you could sit in that seat if you were the first person to say, "Shotgun!"

Every family has its own version and special rules attached to this game. If you were to observe this ritual outside *our* vehicles, you might call our version full-contact shotgun. For our kids, you could call shotgun and even get into the front seat, but you weren't safe and secure until you had your seatbelt buckled. Until that happened, you could be physically removed from the spot.

There was always a battle between my two boys. Mitch, the younger of the two, was a little quicker. But Travis, the older brother, was much stronger. Time and again, Mitch darted into the car and got the spot, only to be thwarted by his big brother, who ripped him from the seat.

On one particular occasion, Mitch found himself thrust into the backseat yet again. He was visibly frustrated. Seeing his downcast demeanor, I turned to his brother, who was comfortably situated next to me in the front, with his seatbelt fastened.

"Travis, why don't you let your brother ride up front this one time?"

Travis thought for a moment then looked at me with a sly grin and said, "Nope."

I realized I could go ahead and make Travis move to the back. Then, out of nowhere, Travis turned to me and, "Dad, what do you think Jesus would do?"

To say I was a proud papa at that point would be an understatement. We had bought our kids the W.W.J.D. bracelets and explained the story of Sheldon's book to them. And here, in the midst of a round of full-contact shotgun, my son had invited a teachable moment.

I turned to Travis and began to talk about Jesus being a servant, giving up the spot of honor at the table, looking out for the needs of others, coming to serve and not to be served. At the end, I told Travis, "Jesus would probably give up his seat in the front for his brother."

Travis, ever thoughtful, looked out the window for a moment before responding, "I don't think so. I think Jesus would let me drive."

Hmm. Teachable moment over.

One of the questions I ask my student leaders is: *What would the world look like if everyone followed your example?*

We learn from the example of others. Then, when we're in situations where we're unsure what to do, we try to make good decisions based on the examples of people we trust and respect. Paul instructs Timothy to live his life as the example of a Christ follower for other Christ followers.

Can you see some of the Six *P*s at work behind the scenes in this passage? Paul doesn't tell Timothy just to be a better person than everyone else. He offers this instruction in the context of a movement that centers on the person of Jesus Christ and the spread of his mission and message throughout the world. Timothy is being called on to set an example that will advance the movement. He is to live this out for a certain group of people—the believers, the ones he has been ordained to lead. These will be the people who will benefit and learn from the example he sets.

Timothy's role is one of spiritual influence. In some ways, it is similar to your role as youth leader. You're involved in the lives of students to make a spiritual difference.

LEADING BY EXAMPLE

Imagine trying to teach and develop leadership within your students yet being unwilling to serve as any type of example for them. The conversation would be awkward.

You: It's important for you to set an example that others can follow.

Student: What do you mean?

You: You know, do the right things for the right reasons.

Student: Can you give us an example?

You: Sure. Look at what Paul said to Timothy.

Student: But that is Paul's instruction. Where's the example?

You: It's something you'll have to learn as you go.

Student: How did *you* learn it?

You: I had some people I respected and trusted live it out in front of me.

Student: Can you show us how to set an example?

You: How about I show you a video on the life of Mother Teresa?

And students walk out of your leadership training hearing a principle but not seeing the picture. You can *be* that picture. Do you lead by example?

I've met the youth leader who tells students to stay off their cell phones during group time but is always on *his* cell phone. Or the youth leader who challenges each student to show up for the service project on Saturday morning but can never make it herself. Or the youth leader who talks about integrity in front of students but lives without integrity behind students' backs. Rather than imagine the names of people who fit these descriptions, a better exercise might be answering the question: *Does that sound like me?*

It's easy to incorporate a *Do as I say, not as I do* philosophy when it comes to our role in the lives of students. But when this happens, it's like watching the air go out of the balloon as it flies around aimlessly and crashes to the floor. This is the kind of example that leads to underlying cynicism and disappointment in both our students and fellow youth workers.

Leading by example means you don't become a walking double standard. Those who say one thing and do another betray the trust given to them and tear away at the fabric of their credibility. Leading by example is also a responsibility. It's owning both your words and actions and making sure they agree.

Youth leaders can inspire others by their example and by their willingness to be the first to act. In this way, you show your students the way by doing it yourself. Once they see it, they have a picture of what it looks like. Then they put themselves in the picture. They start to think, *If she can do it, I can do it.* You are a youth leader when students follow your example. That's a powerful principle and a heavy responsibility. It always makes me think about the kind of example I'm setting.

Let me share a story of the power of example. While it's a story of another youth leader who served in my youth ministry, it could just as easily have been me in similar situations. We all make mistakes, and often we don't live up to the examples we hope to set. But that

53
*

shouldn't become an excuse or a rationalization when we fail in our responsibility.

Adam was one of our youth leaders. He was an older guy who had given a lot of years of volunteering off and on in the youth ministry. He was a fairly successful businessman and felt comfortable in front of a crowd. He often led the midweek teaching.

The last day Adam served on our youth staff was determined by what happened after one of those meetings. He was teaching that night on the fruit of the Spirit. It was a great talk, and the students were deeply engaged in the discussions that followed. After the meeting, we headed to the gym to play some basketball. Adam loved basketball. He wasn't a stellar player, but he was scrappy, and his competitive nature raised the level of his game.

We were about ten minutes into the first game when it happened. Adam had the ball and was driving to the hoop. One of our more uncoordinated freshman students went to defend the basket. In the process, he tripped over the feet of another player and crashed head on into Adam, knocking them both to the floor. Adam jumped to his feet, appearing extremely agitated. He stood over the student on the floor, grabbed him by the back of the neck, and yanked him up.

"What was that?!" he yelled into the student's face. The student looked stunned and was speechless.

Then Adam grabbed the student by the shoulders and pushed him down, hard. Immediately, everyone rushed in to separate Adam from the student. Adam started yelling at everyone around him. I stepped in to try to diffuse the situation. I told Adam to leave. He seemed to regain some of his composure and grabbed his stuff and headed out the door. Then I went over to the student to make sure he was okay. He seemed surprised by the whole thing, but he wasn't hurt and didn't want to pursue any type of action against Adam.

Then, as we were all left in the stunned calm after the storm, one of the other students said, "Man, the fruit of the Spirit must not apply on the basketball court."

We all laughed. And I realized they're not only listening; they're also watching. All of a sudden, the notion of peace, joy, love, patience, kindness, self-control—all of that was cast into doubt and suspicion. When your words and your actions don't agree, they may hear you, but they stop believing and trusting you.

For every Adam moment, there are many more examples of youth leaders who have the strength of character and a firm commitment to do the right things, at the right times, for the right reasons. They invest quality time in thinking and praying through the six *P*s, and it shows in their actions. They realized early on that the process of developing student leaders starts with the youth leader.

As Jesus showed his disciples and Paul instructed Timothy, leading by example is something we can all do, no matter our role, no matter our position. We can all make the choice and take responsibility to be become the picture in our students' minds of the right way to lead. We can all take initiative; we can all make the decision to show the way for our students.

THE STUDENT LEADER

WHAT DO YOU MEAN BY *STUDENT?*

There was a trend that took hold in youth ministry during the 1990s and into the early 2000s. We stopped calling the kids in our youth group *teens* and started calling them *students*. Churches began to identify their youth ministries as *student* ministries. There seemed to be something more relevant about that term. Perhaps we were tired of *teens* being a generic description of the loud and sometimes destructive group of young people who had their own room in the church. This, of course, was a room typically decorated with couches and furniture from secondhand stores, posters of the latest Christian music groups, and a variety of video game equipment. I can't count the number of times I heard members of our church, who were mostly older, wonder out loud about "those teens" when something seemed out of place. Perhaps it was time to re-market our adolescents in a more positive light.

I don't know the sociological data that surrounded this shift. My assumption is that we started calling the youth *students* because they were all in school (or, at least, they were supposed to be). I think we went looking for a more respectable name for our young friends in the academic world. Since our students spent so much time being students, that became the best descriptor we could find. Have you noticed how much the culture inherent in our school systems has influenced the culture of our youth ministries?

We operate our calendars around an academic year. We call our youth students. (Have you ever heard a school refer to them as teens?) We divide our students by grade. We incorporate our programming around school events. We select our student leaders using some of the same models and methods used in our schools.

These observations are not meant to be a judgment on our youth ministries. It's important for the church to be integrated in the life of the community in which we live. But who is influencing whom? Every youth ministry has its own culture. Some of it is shaped from the inside and some from the outside. It's important for us to acknowledge the forces shaping the current culture within our youth—excuse me, student—ministries.

Creating and implementing a student leadership development process must always be mindful of the student. You need to prayerfully and thoughtfully consider the type of student you're developing and what you hope to develop them into. It's not enough to cut and paste the leadership development strategies used in other settings and call it good. While some of the same principles may be taught, it doesn't take into consideration the audience and context of the training. Copying the successful leadership development program from your local school or youth organization can't be your default option. It won't yield the type of student leader we need to develop in the context of our youth ministries and churches.

Placing the word *student* before the word *leader* is more about the process of development than about creating a title. There's a difference between being a leader and being a student leader.

LEARNING

A student leader is a learner. Perhaps we call them students because their main occupation at the moment is school. It's like putting someone's occupation before their name (e.g., Plumber Bob, Professor Mary, or Cowboy Bill). The word *student* is a modifier used to describe a young person's situation. It's also a motive. Being a student means one is studying and learning something. In this case, the student is learning how to become a leader.

Jason was one of my students who loved to soak up anything he could about leadership. I remember talking to him about the power of a leader's vision. He was struggling with how to take the preferred

59
*

future he could see and communicate it to those around him. I invited him to literally paint a picture of what that looked like. So the next time we met, he came back with a picture that would look great on anyone's refrigerator. As he described his painting (his vision), I noticed that he was the only person in the picture. I pointed this out to him, and as I saw the wheels turning, I realized that Jason was starting to figure it out.

I love being a part of those moments; those times when the lights turn on in students' minds and they grasp certain concepts of effective leadership. It's exciting to hear about those moments when they share about how they tried it and it worked. It's equally inspiring to hear about how they put leadership principles into practice that didn't work, but they're able to tell you why and figure out what they learned from it.

Leadership *can* be learned. It can be taught and experienced in such a way that our students get better at it. When it comes to leadership, no one has arrived. There are always new situations, new decisions, new visions that stretch even the most seasoned leaders. If your students are willing, they can improve their leadership IQs over time and with practice.

LABORATORY

One of the benefits student leadership development has over other leadership development programs is the opportunity to experiment in a safe environment. I'm not talking about sterile exercises by students dressed in white coats. It's more about students being given real responsibilities and accountability with the requirement to actually lead something. They're learning to lead *by* leading, while being monitored with certain parameters and precautions.

The student leadership experience is the ultimate laboratory of leadership development. Within this laboratory, they get to experiment with their strengths and their creativity while leading others in a controlled environment.

If you take a look at most student leadership development processes, they include many of the following elements:

a) Student leaders work with an advisor.

b) They function within the context of a school, church, or organization.

c) Students receive training.

d) Their leadership roles typically last for a year.

e) They have limited authority.

The idea of a laboratory helps both you and the student understand the process. Students are learning to lead with certain conditions in place. They're not free to do whatever they want. They learn what it means to lead in harmony with the overall goals and vision of the youth ministry. It's in this context, which often includes some trial and error (because there will be error), that a student learns how to get better at leading. Along the way, the youth leader serves as advisor, supervisor, mentor, model, and spiritual guide.

TODAY'S STUDENT

Student leadership development is personal. It's not one size fits all. An effective youth leader gets to know the unique and special makeup of each student leader. We live in a time when a lot of emphasis is placed on the generalizations applied to each generation. Sociologists and cultural anthropologists identify and distinguish each generation by their overarching characteristics. Armed with this information, some may only see what students are capable of based on a certain generational lens. For those who don't spend time with students, it's easy to attach labels to them without actually getting to know any of them.

There are a lot of books, research, and data collected that's designed to give you an overview of both the positive and negative characteristics of the students you'll encounter in your ministry. At the heart of these

61
*

studies is an assessment every youth leader needs to understand: The nature of what it means to be a student has changed, is changing, and is going to change. This means your leadership development process will be unique because you work with a specific group of students, in a specific context, during a specific time.

The students I work with today are growing up differently than the students I started out with (who are now proud parents of students of their own). The research, the lists, the comparisons with past generations—all are helpful in giving us a handle on what students are like today. In order to engage effectively with our students, we must understand the context in which they are growing up. Contextualization enables us to identify certain fundamental commonalities shared by our students in defining the reality around them. Our students are growing up differently than we did because the world is different.

As you get to know the young student leader who is sitting across the table from you, you'll want to consider the various influences that are shaping his or her context. These can include culture, nature of adolescence, technology, parenting styles, expectations and fears.

Culture evolves and changes. Beloit College publishes a list every year that describes the cultural changes that occurred during the growing up years of each incoming college freshman class (*http://www.beloit.edu/mindset/*). It shows just how much varying generations view the world from different perspectives.

On the latest list, I was once again surprised at what has changed since I was their age. Here are a few examples:

"Don't touch that dial!" . . . What dial?

Amazon has never been just a river in South America.

Faux Christmas trees have always outsold real ones.

Major League Baseball has never had fewer than three divisions and never lacked a wildcard entry in the playoffs.

There has always been internet.

62
*

It's always surprising to see how many cultural icons that existed while I was growing up had disappeared by the time the current class was born. New words have emerged, famous people are no longer famous, and the music I heard growing up is now on classic radio. The experiences that shaped my life are often novel or foreign ideas when compared to the experiences our students face today.

Your leadership development process may stay consistent in principle year after year, but it must change in detail to remain relevant. Look for real-life examples that demonstrate effective leadership practice in today's world. The wisdom of leadership, both past and present, may be timeless and true. But you'll need to find ways to tie those lessons to the situations that occur in your students' world.

Adolescence finds new ways to identify itself. Students rebel against the status quo. The fact that they rebel isn't peculiar; it's what they rebel against that changes. The quest for independence is the telltale sign of moving from childhood to adulthood. Students will push against the norms of the generations before them in order to be unique. In the process of forming their own identities, they have a tendency to rebel against the way we did things and want to do it their way.

There are two types of rebellion you may have to navigate. One is non-conformity (rebelling against fitting into current social norms), and the other is non-compliance (fighting against authority). Both types draw the attention of concerned adults by offending them in some way, and both are attempts by students to assert their individuality by opposing what's already in place. Sometimes it's not as much about rebellion as much as it's a desire to be different.

One of the antidotes for rebellion in our students is developing independence through the challenge of leadership. Leadership requires our students to do something difficult in order to grow for the good of

63
*

others. Students today are more open than ever to being part of something significant.

Another change is the recognition that adolescence is getting longer. We are slowly extending the length of adolescence into one's mid-twenties. *New York Times* magazine did a fascinating piece in their August 18, 2010, issue titled "What Is It About 20-Somethings?" In the article, they offer statistical proof of this phenomenon.

Sociologists traditionally define the "transition to adulthood" as marked by five milestones: completing school, leaving home, becoming financially independent, marrying and having a child. In 1960, 77 percent of women and 65 percent of men had, by the time they reached 30, passed all five milestones. Among 30-year-olds in 2000, according to data from the United States Census Bureau, fewer than half of the women and one-third of the men had done so.

New York Times magazine. Published August 18, 2010

In fact, some of my students who have graduated and moved on would say they didn't begin to feel like adults until they had their first children. I think this validates many of the reasons we need to encourage our students to walk through various levels of leadership development. Maturity is formed through the acceptance of responsibility (it doesn't magically occur after your twenty-first birthday) and consequences of one's decisions. My hunch is that those who engage in leadership development will be better prepared to walk through the milestones listed above.

Technology evolves and changes. We are living in one of the most prolific times in history of technological advancement. The gadgets and gizmos we use are improving at a rapid pace. No longer measuring the greatest inventions by the century, we now see new, life-changing technology appearing by the decade (or in the case of Apple, every year). I remember when I bought my first Sony Walkman. It played cassette tapes. It's amazing to see how quickly the technology we use changes and the way it changes us. And I'm just talking about the short period of time that I've had to observe it.

Technology has added convenience to our lives. Perhaps this is seen most powerfully in the way we communicate with each other. I know I'm dating myself, but I remember when I could make a phone call on a public pay phone for a dime. Nowadays, no one under the age of forty even understands the phrase *Do you have a dime? Call someone who cares.*

The cell phone (and now, aptly named smartphone) is becoming an appendage of the modern-day student. My students no longer pick up the phone to talk. We text. We also leave status updates, we tweet, and we friend each other online.

We must always keep in mind that technology is a tool. These tools can help us. We need to know how to use them because they are what our students use. We can be more creative in our training and teaching. But one thing will always remain true: Face-to-face interactions are still ideal. Relationships are best formed by *being* together. And sometimes the only way you can truly be together is to put the technology away for a little while.

Parenting styles change. Have you noticed how much busier your students are than you were when you were in school? I know I'm often overwhelmed by the schedules my own children have. I don't remember rushing from one event to the next (and having my parents on the sideline for each one). Perhaps it's different now because we are trying to be different kinds of parents than the parents we had. Each generation tries to overcome the mistakes of their parents and give their children what they didn't have.

For example, I am a card-carrying member of Generation X. My generation is identified by names like *latch-key kid* and *baby buster*. In reaction to how our parents raised us (we were often left to fend for ourselves), we parent in a way that reacts against that. As a result, our kids (known as the Millennials) grow up in an atmosphere where we are perhaps overly mindful of and involved in every facet of their lives. Thus, we've instilled in our kids inflated egos, exuberant schedules, and a strong sense of entitlement—which begs the question: *What type of parents will they become in reaction to us?*

Whatever role you play as a youth leader, you cannot separate your interactions with students from the influence of their parents (and family). As parenting styles change, your interactions will need to change in order to integrate with what the family is doing. The implementation of a student leadership development process may be seen as one more thing parents have to get their students to. Their kids are already overloaded with homework, sports schedules, and a variety of other involvements.

It's important to communicate (beyond texting and tweeting) with the parents of your student leaders. They need to know your purposes and the benefits their children will derive from leadership development. The goal is to be on the same team. You want to be seen as a resource, not a liability or detriment to something else they are trying to accomplish as a family.

Expectations and fears do not override potential. Each generation has a unique set of expectations. More and more students are feeling the pressure to do well in school so they can get into college. Students spend an enormous amount of time with tutors and coaches and advisors to give them an advantage over other students competing for a limited number of opportunities. With the expectations set so high, there is also the accompanying fear that one might not measure up. Many students are stressed out and overextended. The pressure to perform and excel can be overwhelming.

Perhaps the greatest leadership tool we can give our students is the ability to properly handle failure and overcome the fear of it. The leadership laboratory must be a safe place for our students to make mistakes and to learn from them.

TIMELESS PRINCIPLES

It's easy to focus on generational differences. But there are a lot of commonalities as well. There are some parts of the leadership development process that are as true today as they were a thousand years ago. I've come up with four timeless principles that are vital to any quality leadership development program and therefore should be kept in mind with any student or student group you're working with.

Relationships are important. The best student leadership development programs make the student the priority. Training and teaching connect with students when they occur in the context of relationship. You can spend a lot of time trying to get information into a student's head. But you'll be able to connect the principles if you take the time to know your student's heart. All the data and research describing today's student is irrelevant if it doesn't help you connect. That only occurs in relationship.

Story is the best way to communicate. People always talk about the limited attention span of students. This is especially true when students are trying to stay focused during a long and drawn-out lecture. Yet I'm amazed that no one seems to have difficulty sitting motionless through a full-length movie. Why is that? Because we love a good story. We are drawn to the elements that make a good story. The open-ended nature of the application of story allows students to see themselves in it. They can extract lessons from a story and compare their own experiences to the story.

Example is the best way to teach. People do what people see. This is going to be the most helpful way for our students to learn. They need to act as apprentices, watching someone else lead so they can turn around and try it on their own. It's the power of modeling at work in our leadership development process. This is why your development and practice as a leader is so crucial to effective training. You need to be leading in front of your students so they have something to refer to. You need to become the picture in their minds when they are wondering how to best lead in a given situation.

Leadership is necessary. The need for leaders is not going away. It is not diminishing. There is always a need for leadership. There is especially a need for good leadership. You are not only preparing them to lead today; you are preparing them for that unique *someday*; for that moment when their experiences and growth will culminate in an opportunity that cries out for them to step forward to lead.

Many of the difficulties we face in the church aren't caused by a lack of spirituality but rather by a lack of good leadership. Sometimes a situation isn't going to be helped by being closer to God but by making a better decision. So many of the decisions we make in our churches don't need more prayer but rather need better leaders to make them.

Running ragged in the wilderness while leading more than a million people, Moses doesn't wear himself out because of disobedience or lack of love for God. As his father-in-law, Jethro, observes, he isn't leading very well (see Exodus 18). He is trying to do everything by himself. Jethro knows that God has appointed Moses to lead God's people out of Egypt and into the promised land. Moses doesn't have time to do the things necessary to lead because he hasn't invested in people to help carry the load. He is caught in a type of paradox: He can't lead because he has stopped leading.

Jethro helps his son-in-law become a better leader. He could stand back during his visit and tell others how proud he is that Moses is busy with the people from morning 'til night. But instead he tells Moses, "What you are doing is not good." And Moses begins to learn the difference between being a worker and being a leader. Because he hasn't been leading the nation of Israel properly, he hasn't been able to provide them with the leadership they need.

WORKER-FACILITATOR-LEADER

Now that we've addressed the student, it's time to take a look at what we mean by leader.

One of my favorite movies is the classic film *The Princess Bride*. Vizzini, the overtly obnoxious and arrogant crime boss, keeps saying the word, "Inconceivable!" over and over again.

Eventually, the sword-wielding Spaniard mercenary, Inigo Montoya, looks at him and replies, "You keep using that word. I do not think it means what you think it means."

I don't know how many times I've quoted that line (with my best Inigo Montoya accent) when I hear someone say a word or phrase over and over in a way that doesn't seem to fit. It rings in my mind again when I observe some who paste the label *student leadership* on anything and everything that gets students involved in the youth ministry. I want to stand up and say, "You keep using that word *leadership*. I do not think it means what you think it means!"

Somewhere along the way, in the ever evolving world of student leadership training, something got messed up. It wasn't intentional. It wasn't even noticeable. We simply stopped training and developing student leaders and started developing and training something else. We still put them together on a leadership team. We take them on leadership retreats and hand out cool t-shirts that have the words "student leader" on them. And we schedule leadership meetings every other week. But somehow, we never quite feel like we have a group of leaders.

In the busyness and crazy schedules of our own lives and the lives of our students, we train our students to do what is *necessary* in our ministries but not what is *needed*.

Let's go back to the story of Ben and setting up the chairs.

The necessary task was easy to identify. There were chairs that needed to be set up. Ben was in charge of the event. This made Ben in charge of setting up the chairs. But if Ben and I are the only ones setting up chairs because it's necessary, it doesn't mean that it's helping Ben be a better leader. My goal with Ben is not for him to perfect the art of setting up chairs. That's a different kind of training. Perhaps it's a necessary training. But it's not what I'm training Ben for.

Thinking back over my many years in youth ministry, I realized at some point that my efforts to develop student leaders weren't working. They weren't becoming good leaders; they were becoming good workers. I didn't feel too bad about it because I needed good workers. It was necessary, as the ministry grew, to get more people involved in the work of the ministry. So I gathered a team of students and assigned them tasks to oversee. I called this group my student leaders. But in reality, they were my committed group of student workers.

I had the greeting team, who shook people's hands and made sure the room was ready when we met. I had the recreation team, who coordinated the games and got the supplies together. I had the administrative team, who sent out notes and made sure we recognized birthdays. Every student had a job, a task to do. But they weren't leaders. They were workers.

Many of us, myself included, have fallen into the trap of gathering students who are interested being involved and calling it the leadership team. But involvement and influence are two different things. While there are similarities, influence goes farther and requires more than involvement.

Part of the reason we like to add the label *leader* to our student workers is that they are in charge of something. But that something is a task—necessary, important, and helpful tasks, in most cases. I'm not against students overseeing some of the tasks of the ministry. In fact, I'm all for it.

There's a powerful picture of leadership in Acts 6. The apostles are the leaders in the early church. The movement is just getting started and is taking a little while to get organized. (Imagine your ministry growing by thousands on a daily basis. That's crazy growth.) At one point, the apostles are waiting tables and delivering food because it is a necessary task. Everyone eats. Everyone shares. And since the apostles are in charge, they take care of whatever needs doing, no matter how menial the task.

Unfortunately, spending all their time passing out food takes away from the time needed to do what they are supposed to do, which is lead. So they find and delegate to other capable men the task of waiting tables and distributing food. They find some workers.

Student workers are necessary. A healthy youth ministry will find ways for students to get involved in doing ministry and not just be spectators. But involvement often gets confused with leadership development. Being a student worker may create the opportunity and desire to grow into a student leader (Acts 6 introduces us to Stephen). But simply doing a task within the ministry isn't leadership.

My first so-called leadership team was called The Crew and was comprised of a rag-tag group of junior high and high school students who applied and were approved to be the leaders in the youth group. We did everything the current how-to-build-a-student-leader program told us to do. I wanted to create a top-notch student leadership program for all the right reasons. I just didn't go about it the right way. I gave them all tasks to do. But each one of them could have carried out their specific assignments on their own, without being asked. Even though I tried to provide room for mistakes and failure in a grace-filled environment, I found that involvement didn't always translate into influence. In fact, as I look back, my most influential students—the ones I would now consider to have been the leaders—never wore the t-shirt or joined the program.

While I expect student leaders to be good examples, I know they won't be perfect. But I quickly found that involvement wasn't providing the motivation to truly lead—to be the ones who set the example. I had official student leaders who didn't show up to events *they* planned, who brought alcohol on retreats, who found themselves walking away from God for a period of time, and who forgot they were supposed to be friendly to the visitors in our group. It was discouraging.

If we're going to develop student leaders, we need to begin to talk about what they focus on. Or better yet, *whom* they focus on. Learning to invest in people requires a different perspective and different motive than simply completing tasks. A student worker can accomplish the tasks assigned without the assistance of others. A student leader can't function as a leader in that kind of isolation. In the process of moving from a student worker who can go it alone to a student leader who is leading by the simple definition that others are following, there's another role. It's a subtle middle ground that some of us (me included) have been fooled by.

Back to moving chairs. In the process of asking Ben where all the other blood drive volunteers were, I hoped for the answer that would provide more help with moving chairs, but that wasn't my main objective. I wanted him to think in terms of developing a team. While this is a great way to begin the leadership conversation, it isn't leader-

72
*

ship development if I'm only concerned with a better way to move the chairs. Between the role of student worker and student leader lies the student facilitator.

The student facilitator has been given the opportunity to oversee a task in the ministry. Instead of doing the task alone, the student facilitator enlists the help of others. At this point, it begins to look a lot more like he or she is a student leader. But the one difference between facilitator and leader is a matter of focus. The facilitator is primarily concerned with the completion of the task.

If Ben calls up some of his friends and they come over and help move chairs, then Ben has moved from being a student worker—doing the task that's necessary—to being a student facilitator—doing the task that's necessary, *with* the help of other people. He got others involved, but he hasn't started leading them yet.

I can sense there might be a little push back at this point. I felt the same way when someone looked at my leadership development program and thought it was improperly named. I had a generous view of what leadership looked like and whom I thought was leading. I grew my program from a bunch of students committed to doing the necessary tasks to fewer students who oversaw the completion of the necessary tasks with the help of others. At some point, we were well organized, but I had yet to produce any leaders from our youth ministry.

There's a tired debate out there about the difference between managers and leaders. I think it's a fuzzy issue and only confuses both descriptions. There's clearly overlap between the two. Most of the folks I know in management have their focus squarely on the people they oversee. They're leading. The difference isn't found in titles or job descriptions; it's in one's focus. This is why I added the role of student facilitator between student worker and student leader. It's a subtle change that involves more people, but the people are only necessary as a way to get the job done.

In the midst of this subtle shift, we offer programs and opportunities that produce organizers, task masters, creative thinkers, planners, and implementers but not necessarily leaders. Granted, many of those attributes are important characteristics in the makeup of a leader, but they don't address the heart and soul of what it truly means to lead.

I'm not saying you shouldn't involve workers *and* facilitators. Both are necessary and helpful roles in a healthy youth ministry. There are a variety of ways to get our students involved and engaged. We can assign students to help plan the calendar, take the pictures, and move the chairs. We can encourage them to find ways to move from spectator to participant in the work of the kingdom. I'm simply asking you not to call those groups your student leaders.

Most student leadership programs function at the worker or facilitator level. By all means, use these programs as an entry point and a testing ground for those who may want to step into leadership. But don't call it leadership. Early on in my youth ministry experience, I implemented programs that got students involved and felt that I'd done my job in developing student leaders. But I wasn't intentional enough. A student leader has followers, not just peers. A student may want to be a leader but isn't until he or she actually leads someone else. A student leader focuses on people who are engaged in doing the necessary task.

A student leadership process is going to work well with a group of students who are committed to influencing the lives of others toward a certain objective. This objective will have something to do with each individual's personal growth and the growth of the collective group toward an ideal future. The focus is on people. Which makes it harder.

It's easy for my students to accept a task assignment and learn how to do it. At our house, we call these chores. It's a responsibility to oversee a task. What's harder to do is change the focus from being responsible for a task to being responsible to a person. *That's* leadership. (It's also called parenting.)

If this sounds similar to some of the ideas we discussed in the first section, then you're connecting the dots. A youth worker can't develop student leaders because that person's focus is only on the tasks. You can't pass along what you don't possess. In your growth as a youth leader (as opposed to youth worker), you'll be prepared to engage in the process that develops student leaders.

By all means, keep raising up student workers and student facilitators. Those are necessary roles, especially as your ministry grows beyond three students. I am always on the lookout for potential leaders. Often, the desire to be involved in some way precedes the desire to be an influence. Some of my best student leaders got their start by walking through student worker and student facilitator experiences. They know what it's like to get their hands dirty and are willing to do themselves what they invite others to do. But like Moses, if they only function in the role of student worker or student facilitator, it will keep them from doing what needs to be done as student leaders.

When I coached Little League, I taught the players what the strike zone was. I told them they should only swing at balls located in that zone and *not* to swing at balls outside that zone. Unfortunately, what I taught them and what the umpires called weren't always the same thing. I remember one game in which an umpire would not call a strike on any pitch above the belt. That's not what I taught (nor is it what the rules taught). I tried to explain to him that by making up his own strike zone, he was actually teaching the players the wrong way to play. Based on his response, I could see that I held no influence over his perspective.

75
*

This is the same thing that happens when we develop student workers and student facilitators and call it student leadership. We end up putting our students in a position of unpreparedness for future leadership positions. Their résumés may say they held a leadership position, but all they did was accomplish tasks. They might have gained some experience facilitating tasks with the help of others, but they never got the chance to develop their leadership muscles.

At the end of my conversation with Ben, I wanted more out of him than finding people to help move chairs. My hope was for him to invest in a group of chair movers. I wanted him to create a team of people who did the necessary task and whom he could influence toward something meaningful and significant. The blood drive was simply a means to a greater end. Moving chairs was a small step in moving closer to his vision.

I probably can't say this enough. You and I *need* student workers and student facilitators in our ministries. In fact, the best leadership development programs will include these areas of involvement. But somewhere along the way, there will be one, two, or however many students mature and ready enough to dive into the deep waters of leadership. It is at that point I hope you have prepared a method and the means by which they can begin to paddle around.

DEVELOP A STUDENT LEADER WHO . . .

Leaders come in all shapes, sizes, personalities, styles, and dispositions. No two leaders look alike. Yet there are some common characteristics we can teach to and inspire in each of the students we invest in. These aren't traits someone must be born with. They can be learned. They can be practiced. They can be improved upon.

I'm a firm believer that effective leaders have to take the time to invent themselves. They have to work on becoming the right kind of people who, in time, will become the right kind of leaders. You can't become a better leader by simply attending a weekend seminar. In fact, most of us who have found ourselves in leadership roles have honed our skills because we were thrown into the fire and had to lead. We learned by trial and error, by imitating the effective examples of others, and by doing what we felt was best at the time. So if leadership can be learned, then what do you want your students to learn in order to become better leaders?

This is more than a question about skills. I would love to stop right there, but I think there's more to it than that. There's a deeper description. There's the description that tells us what a leader does. But there's also the description that shows us who a leader is. I want to know who you are trying to develop these students to be before I need to know what you are teaching them to do.

If I step in to observe your student leadership development process, I'm going to ask you a simple question: *What kind of student leaders are you developing?* The short answer is that you're developing student leaders who look and lead a lot like you do. Remember, they are watching your example. They are learning to lead by watching you lead.

What does your picture of a student leader look like in your youth ministry? In your church? Once you have a pretty good handle on that picture; once you've described the outcomes you hope to achieve through your process, you'll have a better idea of what you're trying to develop. You'll have the first steps necessary to begin to move them in that direction. In a sense, it's similar to the process of putting a puzzle together. You need to see the picture on the front of the box before you start to work with all the pieces.

You know what I'm talking about. Open up a puzzle and pour the pieces out on the table. Pick up a random piece, and what's the first thing you do? You hold it up to the picture on the box to see where it fits in the overall scheme. Without the picture on the front of the box you're at a real loss. The picture on the box helps you get your bearings, no matter what piece you pick up.

It's going to be difficult to know whether your student leadership development process is actually developing student leaders unless you have some idea of what a student leader looks like. It's prayerfully and thoughtfully answering the question: *What are some of the outcomes of my leadership development process, and what must take place for that development to be effective?*

Each of our answers will vary based on context. Yet it's our context that will weave one common characteristic through all our descriptions. Our picture has to be different from the picture of student leaders in a school, work, or community setting. While every student leader is developing his or her influence, we must always lean toward a specific spiritual influence. Ours is the task of raising up spiritual people who use spiritual methods to achieve spiritual goals. Our development tools and training must provide students with the opportunity to identify gifts and abilities that may lie dormant within them and work in co-operation with the Holy Spirit as he unleashes these attributes in their lives.

In studying the lives of great leaders in the church, I've observed that they were people who nurtured their inner lives before they were able to influence the lives of others. They were spiritual people who served as spiritual examples for others. Their relationship with God was a prerequisite to guiding others on a spiritual path.

In high school, I was on the track team for one year. I wasn't very good. I know this because there were always more people crossing the finish line before me than after me. Throughout my lackluster season, my personal goal was to qualify for the finals at the end of each track meet. Before the finals, there were a number of qualifying races to see who the fastest runners were. All the runners competing in an event couldn't race on the track at the same time because there were too many of them. Only the top runners from each qualifying race competed in the finals. While everyone there wanted to win, only the fastest and best prepared were even given a chance to compete for the actual prize.

Before Paul admonishes young Timothy to lead by example, he gives clear direction and explains how a person must qualify to be a spiritual leader. It's not for everyone. He states, "If anyone wants to provide leadership in the church, good! But there are preconditions . . ." (1 Timothy 3:1-2a, MSG).

While everyone may desire to be in a place of spiritual influence, only those who achieve a certain character of heart will be effective in that role. With this in mind, our leadership development opportunities must look for ways to develop the type of qualities that Paul describes and outlines for Timothy. Timothy has already seen these characteristics lived out in front of him. Paul is the example. He isn't asking Timothy to be or do anything beyond his own example. This raises the bar for us as youth leaders. We can only expect to teach these qualifications to the extent we're willing to live them out as an example, modeling them in front of those we lead.

Qualifications are important when we're talking about leading by example. Paul offers this extensive list. He paints a picture for Timothy, explaining what a spiritual leader will look like, both on the inside and on the outside.

If anyone wants to provide leadership in the church, good! But there are preconditions: A leader must be well-thought-of, committed to his wife, cool and collected, accessible, and hospitable. He must know what he's talking about, not be overfond of wine, not pushy but gentle, not thin-skinned, not money-hungry. He must handle his own affairs well, attentive to his own children and having their respect. For if someone is unable to handle his own affairs, how can he take care of God's church? He must not be a new believer, lest the position go to his head and the Devil trip him up. Outsiders must think well of him, or else the Devil will figure out a way to lure him into his trap.

1 Timothy 3:1-7, MSG

I think you'll find Paul's list as relevant today as it was in the first century. Listing the qualities of a leader is a common practice. Yet I would encourage you to give these special attention because these fourteen traits offer an overarching view of someone who is developing spiritual influence.

Well thought of. Spiritual leaders recognize that character development has more value and always precedes the building of a positive reputation.

Committed to his or her spouse. Most students aren't even thinking about marriage, but that shouldn't keep them from maintaining sexual purity now.

Cool and collected. The ability to display quiet confidence, not feeling the need to force a way through life, is an admirable leadership quality.

Accessible. Here we can teach our students what it means to walk slowly through the crowd, listening to and meeting the needs of those around them.

Hospitable. Spiritual leaders are fun to be around and exhibit a welcoming spirit.

Know what you're talking about. Good spiritual leaders should possess the ability to explain their faith and the journey they are on in a way that encourages and edifies the church.

Not reliant on any substance. In a world that is torn by hurtful addictions, a spiritual leader seeks to be addicted to and rely fully on Jesus Christ.

Displaying gentleness. Demonstrating influence that is not pushy but gentle because of the realization that God is in control.

Not thin-skinned. A spiritual leader must be able to properly handle criticism and failure, be teachable, and show emotions while not being over emotional.

Not in it for the money. How spiritual leaders handle their finances says a lot about who they are.

Personally well organized and wise. Spiritual leaders see the connection between their decisions and the consequences of those decisions.

Making family a priority. A spiritual leader practices leadership at home before seeking to influence others.

Not a new believer in Christ. A spiritual leader must be further along on the journey toward spiritual maturity.

Well thought of by those outside the church. As a spiritual leader seeks to be an effective leader in the church, his or her influence will be felt beyond the walls of the church. The church must function in the world in order to effectively serve in the restoration and redemption of the world.

Are you convicted yet? I often wonder what to do with a list like this. The first question I need to ask as a youth leader is: *Are these traits evident in me?* Then I reflect on how I am actually living these characteristics out in front of my students. It's not enough to believe these are the right things to do; I must consider how I put these traits into action. Ask: *Am I behaving like the leader this list describes?* It's important to know what kind of student leader you're trying to develop. Look at this list as a way to begin to identify potential student leaders as well. Are there students in your care who are starting to exhibit some of these characteristics? Are there some who desire to grow and develop in these areas?

Perhaps a list of fourteen characteristics feels a bit overwhelming. I know I feel pretty inadequate when I place my own life up against Paul's list. There's a lot to work on. It's a high standard, and Paul knows it. It takes more than desire to be a good leader. Those who aspire to be spiritual leaders have a target on their backs, and there's a lot at stake.

SUBMISSIONAL

I've been looking for a way to encapsulate Paul's list into a word or phrase that will serve as a guide for both youth *and* student leaders; something that best describes this type of spiritual leadership necessary within the church. I am not interested in simply finding a way to create better organizational leaders. I want to inspire both adults and students to be leaders in a movement. Being a leader in the church has to mean more than being the one to select the color of the carpet. My hope is that a person who embraces the call to lead the work of the kingdom will use those gifts in the context of the church. Not all who aspire to lead in their churches find themselves engaged in advancing the work of the kingdom. It's unfortunate but true.

The leadership style most ascribed to Jesus has been "servant leader." Jesus himself says he came to "serve and not to be served." Yet this spirit of servanthood seems to flow out of something deeper. It's a means by which Jesus embodies what the Father is like. Jesus serves people. Jesus serves because that is what the Father does. The act of service is motivated, even inspired, by Jesus's humble obedience to the will of the Father.

As we look even closer, we see that this submission to the will of the Father serves a purpose. The Father sent the Son to serve as the redemptive and restorative fulfillment of the kingdom of God come to earth as it is in heaven. Thus, the submission of Jesus to the will of the Father was an example of what it meant to live within this new kingdom reality. As the moments leading up to the cross become almost unbearable, Jesus utters the words, "Not my will but yours be done." Jesus becomes the supreme example of one fully connected to the Father and fully committed to the Father's plan.

In a word, he is *submissional.* That's the word I would use to describe the type of leaders we should be. It's the word I would put on the picture of the type of student leaders I'm encouraging you to develop. I would define submissional as *one who submits to God's authority in fulfilling God's mission.* Submission + missional. It defines my posture and approach while declaring my purpose and calling.

To be submissional is to be shaped by one's submission to the authority and anointing of God. The very act of submission influences the type and tone of one's leadership. Like John the Baptist, we say, "He must become greater; I must become less" (John 3:30). This means a submissional leader's style will be one that brings glory and honor to the One to whom the leader submits. The way a person leads is also dependent on the type of mission one is leading. The accomplishment of the mission will determine the tone of one's guidance and direction in the lives of those one leads.

Our students have a strong desire to be part of something meaningful and significant. They want to belong to a story that's greater than their own. To be submissional is to be concerned with what God is calling us to do in our culture and environment. Submissional leaders recognize they're part of a movement, the *missio Dei*—the redemptive mission of God to the world through the work of Jesus.

The student leader who guides others toward overcoming injustice is submissional. The student leader who inspires others to end oppression is submissional. The student leader who serves others and sets the example is submissional. The student leader who influences others to pursue God is submissional.

We live in a period when it's easier than ever to identify the needs of those around us. It feels like we have everything we need at our disposal to meet those needs. It also seems like it's easier to do something about it. We just lack the proper leadership.

Within the last five years, I've had students who have . . .

. . . joined forces with the ministry of Invisible Children to help end child soldiering.

. . . raised money in support of the International Justice Mission to put a stop to child slavery and prostitution.

. . . dug wells in majority-world countries in order to provide clean drinking water for people.

. . . visited orphanages and spent time playing and holding children suffering from a variety of diseases.

. . . started clubs and organized campaigns to enlist people in the fight against hunger and poverty.

Here's what amazes me about each of these stories: It wasn't enough for these students to show up and do the work. They felt like God was directing them to do what they could, but they were involved in something bigger than any one person. They couldn't keep it to themselves. They had to get others involved. It wouldn't take more effort; it would take more people.

84
＊

Paul instructs Timothy to set the example for the believers. But it isn't so the believers can create some type of closed-door country club. God is at work, establishing people who are willing to submit everything to God's kingdom in their lives. Timothy's leadership by example isn't meant to be an exclusive exercise for those already in the church. Timothy is living in communion with God to shape the community he is called to lead. In turn, that community is called to infiltrate the world. The church is God's primary presence in the world, looking for ways to establish the kingdom in places God is already at work.

To be submissional is to be engaged in a humble and yielding relationship with God while also being engaged in a purposeful relationship with one's culture (and the people of one's culture) in order to be salt and light. In this way, submissional is incarnational—God entering fully into the context of our lives, *through* our lives.

I want to develop student leaders in the church who are engaged in this type of missional activity. These are students who are living out the Christian life right under the noses of those whom they lead. They will be able to re-imagine the mission of God in the changing landscape of culture, technology, and context. They will live out this mission, serving as an example that will awaken the imagination in others. The submissional leader will look for glimpses of God at work in the everyday experiences. They are intimately involved in the relational work of listening to God and others.

The submissional leader testifies to the transformative power of God at work in his or her own life and becomes part of the transformative power of God at work in the lives of others. This person humbly accepts a leadership role because of a willingness to responsibly serve God in bringing the kingdom to bear in the here and now.

85
*

SECTION THREE

THE PROCESS

NOT A PROGRAM

At this point, I wonder if some might be disappointed. I imagine a few of you thinking, *I've already read through two sections and you haven't told me how to set up my leadership program yet.*

Here's the deal. There's no program. You can't implement a magic formula and have student leaders instantly appear in your youth ministry. Like many of you, I spent my first ten years in youth ministry picking up books that had the words *student leader* on them. Some were good, others not so good. In my estimation, the good ones didn't promise a program.

Program-oriented leadership training books all seem to follow the same basic outline:

1) We created a successful leadership program in our youth ministry.

2) We wrote a book describing what we did.

3) You buy this book, read it, and implement our program in your youth ministry.

4) Results may vary.

I never felt smart enough to successfully copy someone else's program. I couldn't seem to duplicate the people, the dynamic, the timing, or any of the other factors at work in order to make *their* program thrive in *my* setting. When I put their plans into action, I realized I work with different people, exist in a different dynamic, and face a different set of factors. It was like opening the curriculum in front of your three students and reading the first instruction: *Break into groups of four.*

IT'S A PROCESS

At some point, I realized I didn't need a better leadership training program. What I needed was to create space for students who were ready (perhaps more willing than ready) to start leading. Once I began providing students with the opportunity to lead, the lessons started showing up immediately through their real-life experiences.

The best way to learn to lead is by leading. And by that, I mean focusing on people who are engaged in doing the necessary task. In the context of our youth ministries, the necessary task is all about being the people of God who fulfill the mission of God (submissional). It's in this movement that we create space for our students to step up (in varying degrees) to lead.

I encourage you to allow your students to learn to lead like you learned to ride a bike. You didn't watch a video, read a book, or even role play with others to become a bike rider. You moved from non-bike rider to bike rider by getting on a bike and pedaling. In the midst of that process, you probably had someone else there to hold on to the bike and get you started. You may have had someone cheer you on as you figured out how to balance on two wheels. You knew it was working when you did more riding than falling. In a similar way, we can know we're leading by looking around to see if there's anyone following us. Programs won't give you that kind of immediate feedback because programs don't develop student leaders; people do.

When it comes to developing student leaders, both youth leaders and student leaders engage in a process that is similar to learning how to ride a bike, play an instrument, play baseball, or pretty much do anything else; you have to practice. A student leader better understands what it means to be submissional by *being* submissional. Leadership makes more sense when your students practice it and when they see you practice it. Firsthand experience becomes the curriculum. Leadership lessons are formed through the interactions that occur with the people they lead.

I advocate for a certain kind of process that's based on a certain kind of relationship. If you're just starting out, you'll need to identify a potential student leader or two. That may not seem like many. But it's the perfect amount if it's just you getting this process off the ground. The big question you have to answer at this point is: *Who?*

Most of the student leadership programs I've observed have a formal system to enlist and engage students. You may have been a part of one of these systems growing up, either in your school or your own youth group.

SELECTION BY ELECTION

This is the truest form of democratic government. Election by the people. We create a set of positions that resemble the government we grew up with. The person at the top is the president. Growing up, my denomination even included the position of *youth president* in its manual (the governing document of the denomination). The position always seemed to be filled by an older person. I believe it was prescribed for youth ministries that didn't have anyone to lead and guide the youth group. Next is the vice president. The truth is, nobody knows what the vice president does, but he or she is needed in case the president becomes incapacitated at some point. Then we fill other positions like secretary, treasurer, and various representatives.

Young people are nominated to run for each position, and once the nominations are closed, everyone gets to vote. At the end of the process, the students with the most votes are given the titles and awarded the mantle of leadership. The people have spoken.

ELECTION BY SELECTION

At some point, the adults realized the electoral process closely resembled a beauty pageant or popularity contest. It was also decided by whoever happened to show up to Sunday school on the day of the elections. There were some students who really wanted to serve in a position of leadership but would never get the opportunity until they won over the hearts and admiration of the youth group at the ballot box.

In the spirit of fairness, the adults decided that everyone who wanted to serve should have the same opportunity. It was time to level the playing field. If students really had the desire to serve on the student leadership team, they would need to go through a rigorous application process. If they could survive filling out the seven or eight pages of questions that scrutinized every facet of their personal lives, were able to write inspiring manifestos on their Christian walks, and included references (in triplicate), they were deemed worthy to serve.

In this format, the responsibility of choosing student leaders was placed in the hands of the adults. These adults supervised the process and evaluated the applications. At any point along the way, if a student didn't appear to meet the qualifications that were outlined at the beginning, the adults could always encourage the student to apply again next year.

SELF-SELECTION

This is the most subtle of the three systems. Self-selection occurs when there is no formal opportunity for students to bear the title of leader in the group. It also happens when students don't recognize or respond to the positioned student leaders who have been elected or selected through some formal process.

With no formal system in place, students tend to vie for leadership amongst themselves (hopefully not as intensely as something out of *The Lord of the Flies*). Those with the loudest voices and the most courage may force themselves into the spotlight any chance they get. This doesn't necessarily make them leaders, but it does draw attention.

I remember one student who basically ran the youth ministry when I arrived as the youth pastor. She led the music up front. She decided which activities they would put on the calendar. She was outspoken in small group discussions, demeaning anyone who disagreed with her. She wasn't a leader. Many of the students secretly confided in me that they simply referred to her as "the boss."

A formal election or selection process may not attract the students with influence in your youth ministry. These are the students everyone is watching and listening to. Others take their cues from these students. Students don't recognize the leadership of these students by voting for them. They do it by emulating them, listening to them, and following them. How many times have you seen students with natural leadership abilities and the attention of the youth group? You encouraged them to walk through your election or selection process. Yet they refused for one reason or another.

It could be a combination of personality, charisma, and giftedness. Perhaps their influence spills over from other areas, like school or work or athletics. Whatever the cause, other students quickly recognize this strong leadership potential and may begin to follow. And for some reason, we miss out on the opportunity to walk alongside these students in their leadership development because they weren't willing or able to find a place in our program.

I'm not against having a formal system in place, especially when we're providing opportunities for students to serve as workers or facilitators. But our selection and election processes have the tendency to overlook the potential, especially the spiritual potential, inherent in some of our students who may be ready to step up and lead.

I kept thinking I needed to find just the right program where a student would enter as an involved worker on one end and walk out an influential leader on the other. Yet the answer wasn't found in a program. It came about as the result of a process based on building and investing in a certain type of relationship.

EMERGING LEADERS

Shannon was in her junior year of high school when she approached me with an idea. For many years, her parents had provided foster care for babies waiting for adoption. Time and again, she had been exposed to the stories and situations of wanted and unwanted pregnancies and the trauma many of these young girls faced as they had to make decisions about their babies' futures.

At first, Shannon didn't know how to respond to these young mothers. She hadn't gone through what they were experiencing, yet she felt a connection to them in some way. Shannon told me all the things she was feeling and how concerned she was for these girls, many of whom were her age. She knew she had to do something. Her idea was basic. Once a month she would find a way to offer free haircuts, manicures, pedicures, and other beauty treatments for these young mothers.

I thought it was a great idea. But then I asked her about her skills. "Do you know how to cut hair?"

She responded, "No, but I'm going to find all the people I need to make this happen."

And she did. Shannon got students from a local beauty school to volunteer their time once a month. She raised money for the supplies. She got some of her friends involved (some of whom she bribed with free manicures), and ultimately, Shannon led a venture the most rewarding result of which was relationship building.

Shannon didn't have any experience with this kind of thing. She just jumped in and did it. Who was I to tell her she couldn't?

Do you have a process in place that offers a way for students like Shannon who see a need and want to lead? One of the downsides of creating a leadership program is that students may not feel the inspiration to step in and lead during our election and selection processes. Do they have to wait for next go around, or can we begin to nurture their initiative and tap into their potential when we see the signs?

Sometimes the only thing you need to do as a youth leader is create some space where leadership is necessary. This may require you to step back in certain areas, to release certain portions of the ministry to see who might be willing to fill the void. You might be surprised who is willing to step forward and accept the challenge. Students are looking for a cause to give themselves to. A formal leadership position might not inspire them. But an opportunity to develop a ministry or meet a need may be the very thing they can give their lives to.

A MEANS TO AN END

A lot of students may get involved. Few students have the desire to lead. When students see what's required of the high call of leadership, the many are often whittled down to the few. Every student in your group would benefit from some form of leadership development. But learning about leadership is different from the act of leading. You don't really learn how to lead until you actually lead something. Not every student is willing to pay the price necessary to be a leader.

Most of our leadership programs are closely tied to involvement. Students want to be involved and are often motivated by the recognition that comes from being involved as student leaders. Their involvement comes with a title and gives them a greater sense of credibility among not just their peers but also superiors and adults around them. They see the title and position as a way to be acknowledged and accepted.

What ends up happening is they all get to wear the same t-shirt and meet once a month (with snacks provided). They go through a lesson or curriculum that teaches leadership principles. They discuss all the tasks that need to get done. But they never get to actually lead anything. They get to do a lot of work, and they sometimes get to facilitate a project, but they aren't engaged in regularly leading others in some area of ministry.

This is a real disservice to those students because they don't get the opportunity to develop their influence beyond the titles or positions they hold. They don't get the chance to see how, the minute they make an important but unpopular leadership decision, they have the potential to divide the room. Now they have to learn how to listen well and lead well in the midst of a group of people who aren't all that impressed by the nametags they wear.

I want you to think through the whole process of developing your student leaders, from beginning to end. In fact, I want to encourage you to begin *with* the end. Begin with the picture of what you want your student leaders to look like and what you are hoping for them to actually lead. Then use that as the vision you place before your students. Describe the idea of what they could become and how you will create space in your youth ministry for them to grow and develop into that. Show them where it will be hard. Be honest about the demands of leadership. Keep the bar high and demonstrate the character of leading oneself well.

Talk about the need for leaders in the mission of God. Demonstrate how God has always worked through people to bring about kingdom realities. There is no other plan. We are God's plan, living as God's people. Lay out the expectations of what it means to be a spiritual leader and a submissional leader. Pray with them and for them that God would inspire some of them to step into leadership.

Always keep the need and necessity of leadership in front of your students. Every time you point out where leadership is needed, you will open the door for a handful of students, hopefully eager to be involved. Your role is to help them discover and develop some level of influence through the way they lead.

CHURCH LEADERS

Can I be honest here? I'm tired of our youth ministries and churches copying everything we do in the area of leadership development from our schools and the best business practices of corporate America. Our work in the church needs different leadership training. While some of the principles that make good leadership in businesses, schools, and government may be applicable in the church, we need to train and develop leaders who guide others in the work of the kingdom. Somewhere along the way, spiritual leadership development got hijacked. A leader in the church is often barely distinguishable from other organizations that provide goods and services or solve social problems. We've forgotten that the church is a missional people who need to be led by submissional leaders.

It's been a slow process. Over time we've looked at what works and is successful in other areas and used them in our church. Then, what ends up happening is that we simply keep the cycle going. We do what we learned when we were students in the youth ministry. We define our ministries by the programs we provide. We may call it by a cooler name, but it looks a lot like the experience students can get if they run for student government positions in their high schools.

I want to challenge you to reconsider how you shape and develop student leaders in your youth ministry. If our purpose is to develop submissional leaders (and I know it is)—that is, students who submit to the will of God to fulfill the mission of God—don't you think that will require something different? Won't the training, the instruction, and the preparation look different for this than it would if our students were trying to figure out how to serve as the president of the Key Club?

There will always be certain principles and philosophies that overlap. Good leaders go first. Good leaders believe in their people. Good leaders have a clear vision. Good leaders listen well. The list could go on. But shouldn't our goal be bigger than the development of *good* leaders? Our churches need a unique type of leader. We need submissional leaders.

What I think we've done, at a variety of levels in the church, is continually look outside the church to discover our leadership models and methods. We have operated under the assumption that people who are good leaders in their businesses, schools, and organizations would make good leaders in the church. In a sense, we've selected and elected people who carry their leadership training into the church with them.

What if we flipped this thing on its head? I am constantly challenged with the idea of what it would look like if the church stayed true to the mission of God and trained its leaders accordingly. We should be the ones training submissional leaders who then take this mindset and capability back into the places where they work and attend school. Instead of adopting the models of businesses and schools, we work toward developing a biblical model that produces a different kind of leader. What would it look like if we invested our energy into growing student leaders who lead the church well and infiltrate their schools rather than continuing to develop leaders who lead their schools well and infiltrate our churches? Do you see the difference?

Once again, I recognize the overlap. It's not, nor should it be, one side or the other. I've read a lot of leadership books from both inside and outside the church. Most of them say a lot of the same things. I think it always comes back to thinking deeply about the type of student leader you're trying to develop. You must always consider whether

97
*

your picture is in line with the goal of developing submissional student leaders. You run the risk of missing the mark if your only strategy is to copy the best practices you see out there.

A DIFFERENT KIND OF JOURNEY

If you were to liken the leadership development process of both youth leader and student leader to a road trip, you'd have mile markers along the way to help you gauge your progress. Mile markers give you a measurement of how far you've come and how much farther you have to go. They're also cumulative. Mile marker 85 doesn't exist without the first 84. The leadership journey starts out by learning to lead ourselves. As we begin to lead others, that practice is still important. Each step along the leadership path builds on the previous steps taken.

Mile markers are about the journey, not the destination. Each mile marker is unique. Each exists in a different context and different surroundings. As it relates to your youth ministry, each student is at a different marker on the journey. While you may be traveling in the same direction, they're all at various places, in both spiritual and leadership development. Each step in a student's maturity and growth is something to be acknowledged, nurtured, and celebrated.

Rather than creating a one-size-fits-all model for your student leaders to walk through, I recommend finding ways to work with emerging student leaders at whatever place they're at in their journey. While the direction of our training may be similar with each student, we all move at different speeds. One way the church can differentiate itself in its leadership development is through the particular care and nurture of each individual student. In fact, my recommendation is for your student leadership development to look a lot more like a discipling relationship.

Nothing new here. This isn't even my idea. All I know is that the pages of Scripture are full of examples of leaders who were nurtured, developed, and cared for by others along the way. The relationship between Paul and Timothy is an ideal picture of a leader developing another leader and one we have already examined and discussed for other reasons. One on one. Both of them traveling along on their leadership journeys. Paul, speaking from his experience and insight into the situations Timothy is facing. Timothy, putting the lessons of leadership into practice and serving as an example for the next generation of leaders who will follow in his footsteps.

It's been the way of the church since its beginning. We invest in people. We engage in conversations. We pass on what we learn to the next group. We grow reliable people who will take what they learn and pass it on to others (see 2 Timothy 2:2).

One of the barriers to effective leadership development in the church is that we've equated growth with *numbers*. In our attempts to grow the youth ministry numerically, we've become too busy to go deeper with a few key individuals. In an effort to be more efficient, we've created a structure and programs to equip the masses. But it hasn't produced the results we hoped for. It hasn't developed the kind of leaders we need.

A program is a manageable system. Personal relationships are messier. They take more time. Programs are easier to control. There are specific parameters. You know when you meet. You know what you talk about or train on. You know when the program is over. Personal relationships—the discipling kind—don't always abide by the rules. They take longer and are more intensive. Each one looks a little (or a lot) different, so they're harder to prepare for. People have been trying to write the curriculum on relationships for a long time. Unfortunately, the only real way to learn is to experience them with someone else. If you think it's difficult to copy a successful program, you should try copying a successful relationship.

If we view leadership development in our ministries as the process of creating and growing discipling relationships, it will inform and shape the way we go about developing each student. A discipling relationship recognizes the role of youth leader as mentor—one who teaches through his or her example. It gives the student the opportunity to apprentice—to learn to lead by leading. It is through the act of living life together that students can observe how the youth leader leads and the youth leader can see how the student leads.

MENTOR

Paul has a unique father-son relationship with Timothy. He continually communicates his care and concern, greatly interested in how Timothy is faring in his pastoral role. Paul calls Timothy his "true son in the faith" in the opening words of his first letter (1 Timothy 1:2). His second letter opens with a similar greeting of love and affection as he recounts how he thinks and prays for Timothy "night and day" (2 Timothy 1:3). This whole relationship has a much different feel from your typical training program.

Who can forget the relationship that develops between Danny Laruso and Mr. Miagi in the original version of the movie *The Karate Kid*? (What?! You've never seen it? Where have you been?) More than teaching Laruso about karate, Mr. Miagi uses the pain and realities of life to teach Danny how to be a man. The movie powerfully illustrates the role of nurturer in the life of a young teenager. In the character of Mr. Miagi, we see a grace giver fleshed out. He does not demand. His own life becomes open for Danny to find what's most important in life. In the end, Danny comes out on top.

As the movie comes to its dramatic close, you find yourself cheering over Danny's victory. More than defeating a cocky kid from the enemy dojo in a karate match (yes, I gave away the ending...but you've had twenty-plus years to see the movie!), you realize his greatest opponent has been the obstacles he carried in himself. And when the victory is sure, young Laruso having discovered the elusive balance he has sought, the final words of the film ring out above the applauding crowd: "We did it, Mr. Miagi. We did it!"

The camera freezes on a short Asian man who seems to be standing head and shoulders above the crowd; his face is beaming. He is Mr. Miagi. The model. The molder. The mentor. The nurturer.

I once heard a story about Albert Einstein, who, toward the end of his life, removed the portraits of two scientists—Newton and Maxwell—from his wall. He replaced them with portraits of Gandhi and Schweitzer. When asked why, Einstein explained that it was time to replace the image of success with the image of service. Einstein understood that he needed some new examples in his life.

Are you willing to become the example in the life of one of your student leaders? Are you willing to step into this kind of discipling relationship, this type of mentoring role? As we grow and develop as youth leaders, we invest in others so they in turn can do the same.

Paul has taught Timothy, both in word and in action. Now it is time for Timothy to pass those things on to others.

APPRENTICE

Adolescence is a key decision-making time. Students begin to chart the course of their lives not only in the area of occupation but also in personal habits, character, and relational skills. This is not a period of time when we can sit back and hope for the best. It is a season of growth like no other. The transition from childhood to adulthood is the laboratory for discovering what we will pack in our suitcase for the journey of life. We cannot wait until they reach adulthood to begin the process of developing leadership skills.

People have been passing down skills and knowledge from one generation to another through various forms of apprenticeship for years and years. Working alongside someone with a recognized area of expertise was the prerequisite to stepping into a similar role in society. Those who were being apprenticed often had to produce their craft or skill alone to prove they had *mastered* their training.

In the relationship between Timothy and Paul, young Timothy serves in the role of apprentice. This isn't a situation where Timothy moves into Paul's house and serves under Paul's guidance until such time as he can branch out on his own. While Timothy and Paul do spend time together, Timothy has a job. Timothy is already doing the work of a submissional leader in the newly planted church in Ephesus. He is earning while he learns. We might call this a type of on-the-job training. In the classic sense of apprenticeship, Timothy serves as a *journeyman*, possessing the basic skills necessary to do the job but still under the watchful eye of his mentor.

Perhaps it was the busyness that pervaded our lives toward the end of the twentieth century that slowly eroded the mentor-apprentice model. The rapid pace of our society has forced us to provide more in less time and with better packaging. Our youth ministries are bursting with activity. But it's not necessarily the type of activity that creates the space necessary to grow submissional leaders. We can't simply hand students a leadership manual with all the answers in the back, like a travel agent telling people how much fun they're going to have on their trip. Youth leaders must be the tour guides who walk alongside and point things out, discovering what works and wrestling with the issues of life together.

LIVING LIFE TOGETHER

Paul and Timothy walk through the ups and downs of life together. It is a special and unique relationship. Timothy not only learns under the tutelage of Paul; he becomes an extension of Paul's ministry. There is a connection there. A reciprocal admiration and respect for each other.

Recalling your tears, I long to see you, so that I may be filled with joy. I am reminded of your sincere faith, which first lived in your grandmother Lois and in your mother Eunice and, I am persuaded, now lives in you also.

2 Timothy 1:4-5

I'm inviting you to commit, as a youth leader, to enter into a strong and significant relationship with your student leaders. This will require spending time together. It will mean letting them see behind the curtain, exposing them to parts of your spiritual journey. They will learn by the example you set. They will draw leadership lessons from watching you lead right in front of their eyes. They will see where you do well and where you make mistakes. They will see your struggles. In turn, you will watch them and guide them in their growth as submissional leaders.

Student leadership in your youth ministry can't be another program. It is more about creating space for students to wrestle with the possibilities of leadership. I've observed that the best student leadership development happens in the context of relationship.

It's personal. It takes time. It looks different for each student.

I remember sitting across from Josh, a plate of French fries on the table between us. We spent the better part of an afternoon talking about what was happening in Josh's small group. A few months earlier, I had given Josh the opportunity to lead a group of four freshmen who wanted to go a little deeper in their spiritual journey. It was a perfect fit for Josh and his leadership abilities. That's not to say things went perfectly.

There were all kinds of issues Josh was facing with his guys. We didn't talk about what Bible study curriculum to use or how Josh might better teach on a certain topic. This conversation was all about the relationships Josh was building with his freshmen. He had a lot of questions. Some questions I had answers for. Other questions left us both brainstorming about what some good next steps might be.

This wasn't a conversation that occurred because it was part of the next lesson. Josh's leadership—really leading his guys—was the lesson. I was there to listen. I was there to find out what Josh was learning and to point out the lessons he might be missing along the way. I was there to encourage Josh. As we prayed together, I heard Josh's heart, and he heard mine. We were both devoting our lives to being submissional leaders. I was leading Josh, and Josh was leading his freshmen.

There is a pretty common saying about certain things being more "caught than taught," and it certainly applies to leadership. People may doubt what you say, even forgetting the lessons you teach them as a youth leader. But they remember what you do, and they often emulate it. The question is, in a discipling relationship, what are your student leaders catching from you?

LEVELS

While I am wary of adopting a cut-and-paste model when it comes to leadership development, I do find it helpful to identify ways to measure progress. There are mile markers on our roads for a reason. They help us know where we are in the journey.

The picture of the submissional student leader helps us characterize the type of student leader we're developing. Now we need to find some ways to describe where we are in the process. I have identified five levels to outline growth in leadership potential and capability, especially as it relates to leadership in the church. Each of these levels builds on the previous one. This means that each remains important in the implementation of the levels that follow it. It's not like a student will achieve success in one level and then move on to the next one. You never *complete* a level; you simply expand and grow in your leadership skills to include the next level. It's like building a house. The foundation is built first, yet it remains important and necessary when you move to the next phase of building walls. It's part of the house through the whole process.

Before we look at each of the levels I need to make an observation (it's more of a warning). There are five levels, and they all begin with the letter *P*. I promise you this wasn't intentional. It may appear I have a strange affinity for grouping words that begin with the same letter. Chalk it up to coincidence. As I was involved in editing each section, it suddenly hit me I had provided two lists of words, each word beginning with the letter *P* (and one of those lists is actually called The Six *P*s). At this point, I'm wondering if a better subtitle for this book might have been, *How to Organize Your Student Leadership Development Process Using Words that Begin with the Letter* P. Hopefully you're willing to let this slide. After this list, no more *P* words. I promise profusely. Let's move on.

A youth leader serving in a mentoring role can discern the level of readiness of a student leader for more expanded leadership roles using the following levels:

1. **Personal leadership. Teach students to lead themselves first.** Every person needs to learn how to lead at this level. This is the foundation. It's where a person develops his or her character. Paul commands Timothy to "hold on to faith and a good conscience" (1 Timothy 1:19). He also instructs him to "watch

your life and doctrine closely" (1 Timothy 4:16). Most people disqualify themselves for leadership because of poor decisions, moral failure, or sinful choices. No one is immune from the temptation to live one way in public and another way in private. But, for the submissional leader, partial obedience to God's best isn't obedience but convenience. In fact, as one moves through each of the levels, leading yourself first becomes more crucial.

2. **Peer leadership. Teach students to learn to live as examples to those around them.** As student leaders show consistency in character and spiritual growth, they may begin to develop a greater influence over their peers. Their example begins to have an effect on others in the youth ministry. They are recognized for their faithfulness to the Christian journey. They earn the respect of their peers. Their example becomes one that others point to and seek to emulate.

One of my favorite times in youth ministry is when we get to a place on a retreat or at a camp where students feel comfortable enough to open up about what's really going on in their lives. It was during one of these times, sharing around a campfire, that I recognized the impact of one of my students named Kristi. In the midst of the sharing, I noticed that Kristi's name kept coming up again and again. As different students shared, they kept referring to Kristi as an encouragement and role model and good example. When we were walking back to our cabins, I pulled Kristi aside and asked her how she felt about all she heard. I could tell she was a bit taken aback. She said, "I had no idea they looked at me that way."

This is a level of leadership that doesn't rely on position or a formal role. Student leaders (even if they don't see themselves as leaders at this point) are influential because of the way they live. The way they lead themselves goes public.

3. **Positional leadership. Occupy a more formal role that recognizes leadership.** The first entry point into leadership for students typically comes in the form of a recognized position. Like I said earlier, a title doesn't make you a leader. But oftentimes, a leader will be given a title. A position provides a platform. A position is often the reward for recognized leadership in both the personal and peer leadership levels. A position may offer resources that previously weren't available to the leader.

   The true test of leadership at this level is what a student leader does after he or she has been given a position. How a student leader handles authority and responsibility will affect the willingness of others to follow along. Some student leaders may assume that serving in a position of leadership automatically earns them the support and loyalty of others. That's just not the case. A position only buys a person time to show what type of leader he or she will be. Positional leaders who demand support rarely get it. But positional leaders who inspire others will typically get the support they need.

4. **Programmatic leadership. Students lead a portion of the ministry.** Some may wonder why I would include a programmatic level when I've, up to this point, been so clearly against student leadership *programs*. I'll clarify this by saying I think developing student leaders is a process, but we should allow student leaders to lead various programs. If you've created a program to involve students as student workers or student leaders, this may be a potential area for a student leader to oversee.

   A great example of this is Ben, the one I encouraged to lead all the chair movers. His role as a student leader involved oversight of a variety of community service opportunities. Ben had responsibility and accountability for an entire area of the ministry. If Ben didn't lead it well, it didn't go well. Ben led other students in carrying out the duties and assignments of this particular area.

5. **Pastoral leadership. Students assume a role of spiritual authority in the youth ministry.** I consider this to be the highest level of leadership recognized in the church. This student leader shows a unique interest and sense of mission to serve the church in pastoral ministry. There is a special sense of anointing and willingness to equip others in the church for service. While a local congregation may identify certain gifts and graces necessary for pastoral leadership in a student leader, each church has a different ecclesiology (study of the role and function of the church). The path and preparation student leaders must take will depend on their particular church structures and governances. When student leaders reach this level, they may consider moving into a mentoring relationship with one of the pastoral staff.

Typically, students who sense a call into some type of pastoral leadership in the church will devote some time to intensive preparation and study. While not everyone will go to a seminary or Bible college, it is important that our pastoral leaders be properly equipped for this type of service to the church.

The process of developing student leaders is not only vital for today; it's an investment in the future of the church. The quality of student leaders you develop at the high school and college levels has a direct impact on the quality of leaders they will be when they step into more influential roles of leadership.

I remember coming home from a Little League coaches' clinic put on by the local high school baseball coach. This guy knew what he was talking about. He'd been coaching since 1972. At the start of the clinic, he looked all the coaches in the eye and told us something I hadn't really thought about before. "Our high school baseball program has improved because the local Little League program has improved. The success of our team and the caliber of our players are directly impacted by the quality of coaching and training these kids receive at the Little League level."

Wow. I suddenly felt a little bit of pressure. Now I'm realizing how important the fundamentals are, how important it is to do the right things the right way. I guess that's why I'm so invested in raising up quality student leaders. These students will one day lead the church in a variety of capacities.

GUIDELINES

As you think through your unique strategy and process, consider the following guidelines. These will help you think through your philosophy (one of the six *P*s) and may cover an area you haven't considered yet.

1. **An entry and exit point.** Consider the various ways students may enter into this type of discipling relationship. Will you draw from those who demonstrate a willingness to serve in student worker or student facilitator roles? How will you celebrate growth? Are there certain points along the way when students may step away from leadership if they desire?

2. **Combination of teaching, action, and reflection.** Students learn to lead by leading. You may also have certain insights and lessons that will guide and direct your student leaders in the situations they currently face. One of the things I teach every student leader is what I call my Event's Not Over lesson. It basically goes like this: *An event's not over until a) everything is put*

away; b) everyone who helped is thanked; and c) you've evaluated the event. This lesson teaches them the importance of following through to the end, being grateful, and learning from their experiences.

3. **Room for failure and making mistakes.** This one is huge. To create the space necessary for students to lead, they must be allowed to fail and make mistakes in that space. All of my experience has taught me that students will actually learn more from the mistakes and failures they experience then they will from the successes. While we don't wish for failure, we certainly use *certain* failures and mistakes as valuable lessons in our leadership training.

4. **Integration into the life of the church.** If we are training our students to be submissional leaders in the church, we must integrate what we are doing into the life of the church. There are a variety of ways that our leadership experiences can take our students beyond the walls of the youth room. We want our churches to recognize our students as leaders in the church, not simply in the youth ministry.

5. **Not dependent on one person.** The best job description I've ever heard for a leader is that a leader develops other leaders. If you are the only one entering into a discipling relationship with your students for the purpose of training and developing leaders, then perhaps it's time for you to raise up more youth leaders. The reason for this is simple: What happens if you're no longer there?

6. **Interactive & engaging (participate rather than spectate).** Once again, leadership development isn't just another chance for you to teach a lesson. Leadership is a hands-on activity. While there will be moments when you find yourself in front

of a white board or going over a handout, you must continually prepare and engage your students in the real work of relationship building. Your best lessons will come from those moments when they are able to observe and learn from your leadership example and you are present to observe and offer feedback from their leadership efforts.

7. **Connected to real-life moments and application.** Remember those moments in school when you asked the teacher if something was going to be on the test? A better question might have been, "Am I ever going to use this in real life?" (Most of the time this question is muttered when a student is facing an onslaught of homework.) The same rings true with your leadership development. If you allow students to learn about leadership by actually leading, they'll figure out quickly what works and what doesn't. The best curriculum flows out of the real-life experiences both you and your students face in the midst of leading others.

CULTURE

One of the main reasons I think a lot of programming efforts fail in our youth ministries is that we haven't created the underlying culture to sustain them. This may also account for those youth ministries that have effectively applied principles or procedures they've learned from others. Cultures have a way of determining what is acceptable and what isn't.

For example, I don't think a friendship evangelism campaign will take root in a youth ministry that hasn't already done the hard work of creating a culture that values evangelism in a variety of forms. So the youth pastor who returns from a conference, having experienced the powerful impact of the Evange-Cube, will face a great deal of hesitation, if not flat out resistance, if the youth ministry doesn't have a culture that values and practices evangelism.

You will face similar resistance if you start to create strong, discipling relationships with your student leaders and you haven't created the culture that understands and supports that.

In my last position as a youth pastor, I made a strong case for engaging our students in more ministry activities and fewer social (fun and games) activities. I was immediately met with apprehension and found myself under the scrutiny of a small group of parents. They were used to a youth ministry that provided a whole calendar full of social activities for their students to be engaged in. They didn't appreciate the change. I was not only facing a different mindset of what it meant to be an effective youth ministry; I was facing a culture that existed long before I ever arrived as the youth pastor.

Every youth ministry has a distinct culture. Each culture has underlying values that will attract or repel people. The vocal parents I mentioned above were seeking to protect a certain type of culture that had been embedded into the youth ministry. It supported their expectations. Any attempt to alter or change that culture was met with resistance. In fact, my initial efforts resulted in some parents threatening either to have me removed or move their students to another youth ministry.

Not only is this true for parents, but it's true for students as well. It's difficult to create a youth ministry culture that's welcoming to new people if your current students don't recognize the value of that. A youth ministry culture isn't necessarily visible or even talked about (like it should be), but it certainly is felt when someone tries to make any type of changes that go against it.

Have you ever noticed how water responds to a pebble being dropped into it? Ripples form, in concentric and ever widening circles.

112
*

Yes, the ripples get smaller as they disperse, but they do grow. Within your youth ministry, you are the pebble. While your impact is greatest closest to you, your behavior will impact culture more directly and in greater ways than you realize.

Every culture has certain elements that make it distinct. If you are going to make leadership development a priority, even a key descriptor of your youth ministry culture, it must become evident in the following elements:

A. **Language.** This must be something not only *you* talk about but that your students and other youth leaders talk about as well. When you begin to use the same phrases and terminology regarding leadership development, you'll know it's becoming embedded in the culture.

B. **Traditions.** Figure out ways to honor and recognize leadership on a regular basis. It could be in the form of weekly, monthly, or annual experiences that keep leadership development alive in the rhythm of your youth ministry.

C. **Social Norms.** Like culture, social norms are somewhat unspoken yet realized by those who are familiar with the group. Think about the types of behaviors your student leaders can engage in without prompting or permission. These are the actions both youth leaders and student leaders do in your youth ministry simply because that's the way you do things.

D. **Rituals and Ceremonies.** Build in certain rites of passage that become doorways for students to walk through. Like earning your driver's license, these become ways to elevate the value of leadership above simple habit or going through the motions. Every culture creates ways to honor and recognize the people who are engaged in the activities we value most.

113
*

E. **Symbols.** Symbols are a way we ascribe meaning and significance to visual objects. They help tell our story. They serve as reminders of what's most important and what we don't want to forget. Consider the types of symbols that are visible in your meeting spaces.

F. **Heroes.** As a culture continues to grow, there are certain people who embody the values of that culture better than others. We recognize both their achievements and their efforts. A hero is typically someone who has served the needs of others above his or her own. It is a title appointed by the people. Find ways to identify the heroes in your youth ministry and tell their stories to others, even after they've moved on from your group.

G. **Attitudes and Beliefs.** Cultures are shaped by the attitudes and beliefs of the people who embody them. Thus, the creation of a culture that values leadership development will attract students who identify with or want to be a part of that type of culture. It will draw the students who want to develop their leadership skills.

114
*

Laying the groundwork for a leadership culture may be the first thing you need to do before you start building your discipling relationships with potential student leaders. When you choose to create a youth ministry culture that values student leadership, you are making a decision about both values and the priority of those values. If your current culture doesn't support or value student leadership development, you will need to lay the groundwork in order to make this transition. Here are some practical ways you can begin to implement leadership development into your current culture.

1. Create an environment that both aesthetically and explicitly speaks to the value of leadership development.

2. Begin to point students toward equipping opportunities both inside and outside your youth ministry that will strengthen their leadership capacities.

3. Talk about the value of leadership. Use leadership examples when teaching and speaking.

4. Create and deliver Bible studies on topics that have to do with leadership principles found in Scripture.

5. Model your leadership in front of students and be vulnerable about what you're learning and growing from in your own leadership journey.

6. Begin to make the development of student leaders necessary for your youth ministry to grow and move forward.

7. Reward leadership when you see it.

8. Begin to find ways to measure the leadership capacities of your students. Acknowledge growth when it is displayed.

9. Begin to train other youth leaders to build effective discipling relationships with students.

10. Find ways to assist parents with developing the leadership skills in their own students.

If it's stated up front that you value leadership development in your youth ministry culture, there will be moments when that claim is tested. One of those tests will come when people outside your youth ministry come to you with questions about something your student leaders have done. If you have truly given students the authority to lead, then they must also take responsibility for the consequences of their leadership. If someone comes to you with a question about something your student leaders are leading, send them to the students. Many adults will try to shortcut or sabotage your process by going directly to you. You will break down the process if you don't acknowledge their leader-

115
*

ship in front of others. If you give authority but don't also give responsibility, you have simply allowed your student to serve as a figurehead.

Another test may come from the leadership in your church. Some may feel it is the job of the youth pastor and youth leaders to lead everything. They might be hesitant to put leadership responsibilities in the hands of students. With this in mind, it will be important to make sure you set parameters and minimize any areas of major risk. This is not an effort to transfer leadership from the adults to the students in the ministry. You, as the youth leader, are still leading the student leader. This is an effort to create leaders in training, mentoring those who are being apprenticed in leadership. Of course, if you haven't heard me say this yet, *the most effective way to learn how to lead is to actually lead something.*

Perhaps the greatest challenge to developing student leaders is figuring out how to handle the risk of failure and mistakes. The question is: How much of a risk are you willing to take or allow?

ROOM TO FAIL

Let me say it again: Students learn to become student leaders by leading something (is there an echo in here?). They will need to engage in the very act of leading—focusing on people who are involved in completing the necessary task. Even if you spend an enormous amount of time preparing students for leadership, you'll never know what kind of leaders they will be until they start leading. And, like most things, they won't get it perfect on their first try (or their second).

So the question is, how will you create a leadership culture that gives students the opportunity to lead yet also provides the space for them to fail and make mistakes? We're not just talking about setting up chairs in the wrong configuration. We can fix that quickly, and no one needs to be the wiser. This is leadership. When a leader makes a mistake, everyone who is following the leader feels it. In fact, one of the biggest arguments against instilling the value of leadership in your youth ministry culture will be the concern over the consequences that may occur because of a student leader's failures or mistakes.

I only bring it up here because this is an area that can derail your process if you're not ready for it. You don't have to go *looking* for failure. You simply need to be prepared for it when it happens. Because a youth ministry culture that doesn't know what to do with failure will dumb down the leadership development process in order to minimize the mistakes made by students in leadership training. Perhaps it's because people are afraid of failure or don't know how to handle it properly. Simply hoping failure doesn't happen is not a good strategy. In fact, avoiding failure and the inevitable mistakes that will occur can actually diminish the effectiveness of your leadership development process.

Most people don't like to deal with failure because it's messier than success. That's why we'll invest in a clean-cut leadership development program that teaches our students about the skills, perspectives, and character that are necessary for leadership, but we're hesitant to put them into real-life situations where those factors will be tested. You will go up against a parenting style that wants to protect more than they're willing to prepare.

This is why I like the idea of creating a leadership laboratory. In a lab there are controls in place to keep the experiments in check. Those who work in a laboratory track and measure what works and what doesn't. They're actually able to make progress through failed attempts. They expect to fail. Failure helps remove contingencies and validate theories. Failure is information. We label it failure, but it's more like, *This didn't work, I'm a problem solver, and I'll try something else.* While people are often disappointed by failure in a laboratory setting, they aren't derailed by it.

117
*

In a youth ministry culture that values leadership, within the guiding oversight of a discipling relationship, students are handed varying levels of responsibility that require leadership (not just working and not just facilitating). It might be safer, quicker, and easier if the adults led this responsibility themselves. But that's not the purpose of this process. This is an opportunity to develop leaders because leaders are both important and necessary. This is part of our mission. The formula is simple: Responsibility plus risk equals reward.

There is always some level of risk when it comes to leadership. If we're honest, we run the risk of failure and mistakes at all levels of leadership in the church. No leader is immune. For that reason alone, we must focus on helping our students know how to best handle situations that don't turn out as expected because they messed up or made a poor decision.

I wish I heard more youth leaders talk about this. I think we're afraid because we've seen so many people have to step down from leadership positions in the church because of some type of moral failure. I'm not talking about sinning. That's not the kind of failure I'm addressing here. I'm thinking about the time when Bobby forgot to bring the grill to the youth group cookout. Or the time Susie didn't communicate with parents that the retreat included skydiving. It's the mistakes and failures that come from a lack of experience. Some of it can be avoided. Some of it we have to learn from. That's why I recommend you create a philosophy of failure in your student leadership development process. If you're not comfortable with the word *failure*, then use the word *mistakes*.

LET'S QUESTION FAILURE/MISTAKES

1. **Are you willing to let your student leaders fail/make mistakes?**

   I don't wish for failure, but I don't hide from it either. They're *student* leaders. This means they're learning. They're going to try some things that will probably be less than perfect (great, average, poor, disaster). And they definitely won't happen like they would if I were in charge. It's also important to remember that they learn from both success and failure, but the lessons learned from failure or mistakes are remembered longer. I love it when an activity or event goes well. But if the priority is leadership development, then we'll leave room for failure and mistakes; not big ones but the little ones that come from a lack of experience and perspective. Students will remember the lessons from their failures long after they've forgotten about the effort it took to be successful.

2. **What types of failure/mistakes will you allow? What types will you not allow?** For example, any activity or event that might put people or your church at risk should be avoided. You might also want to keep an eye on how your student leaders handle and spend budget dollars. You may find that a student's leadership is actually hurting the ministry or lowering the involvement of other students. If that's the case, you'll need to find another place for that student to serve. Also, you need to decide what failures or mistakes aren't going to be tolerated, ever. Moral failure, causing harm to others or yourself, character issues, and anything that goes against the policies of your church are the types of behaviors that immediately disqualify someone from leadership. We may initially assume our students already know these things. But we must be explicit with them and clearly outline the difference between mistakes we learn leadership from and mistakes we have to leave leadership over.

3. **How will you explain the possibility of failure/mistakes by student leaders to your church leadership?** There is a philoso-

119
*

phy of success that has permeated our churches. If our purpose and process is the development of submissional student leaders, preparing to serve and guide the church in expanding capacities, we must be willing to give them room to develop. Communication at the start of this process with the senior leadership of your church is vital. Don't surprise them with this. Take some time to lay out what you are hoping to accomplish and the parameters you have put in place. While you aren't hoping for failure or mistakes, let them know you are planning for it.

4. **How will you prepare your student leaders for failure/mistakes?** Your student leaders are going to be afraid to fail. This may keep them from making decisions or moving forward. Your role is to alleviate some of that fear. You can share from your own experience and assure them that mistakes are part of the process.

5. **How far are you willing to allow student leaders to fail/make mistakes before you step in?** Your philosophy should differentiate between the areas where you'll give students more room to fail and areas where you'll step in quickly. My co-worker Kenton told me about a time in high school when he was in charge of a city-wide crusade. The crusade went really well. He planned it all out and involved a lot of people. It was a student leadership success story. The following year he planned to do it again. But this time, he dropped the ball. He waited until the last minute to make some of the important arrangements. As he ran into difficulty after difficulty, he asked the youth pastor to help. The youth pastor not only turned him down; he shut it down. With such late notice it was destined to be a disaster. Kenton was devastated. Fortunately, after letting Kenton think about it for a week or two, the youth pastor came back and encouraged

120
*

him to walk through the process of planning the crusade again. Kenton agreed and ended up doing a lot of the things that made the first event successful. This time went better. It served as a great reminder to Kenton (who works with student leaders now) about maintaining a healthy balance of knowing when to step back and when to step in.

6. **What process will you use to evaluate and learn from failure/ mistakes with your student leaders?** Student leaders who don't ever fail or make mistakes probably aren't learning anything. They are succeeding to the level of their competence but aren't being pushed to try something new or attempt a new challenge. If student leaders are afraid of failing, it will have a direct impact on their ability to lead. They may make decisions that ensure they don't look bad. They may avoid any situations where they can't control the outcome. With that type of mindset, they won't be able to lead; they'll only be willing to acquiesce to the path of least resistance.

ANSWERING THE CALL

121
*

I love the relationship exhibited between Paul and Timothy. You can sense Paul's concern and careful consideration of Timothy as a growing leader. There's another example of this type of relationship in the Old Testament. It's lived out in the lives of Samuel and Eli as told in the opening pages of 1 Samuel.

Samuel is dedicated to God's service before he is even born. His mother, Hannah, sees him as a precious gift. She can see nothing better for him than to give him back to God for God to use however God sees fit. He is an example of a submissional leader from a young age— dedicated to the will of God and called to serve in the mission of God. Hannah gives Samuel back to God and places him in the care of Eli, the priest at the temple. Samuel lives with Eli and grows up under his mentoring and spiritual guidance.

In 1 Samuel 3, young Samuel is sleeping in the temple near the Ark of the Covenant, and the Lord speaks. Thinking it is Eli, Samuel runs into his room and wakes him up. Eli states that he didn't call out to the boy. Samuel goes back to bed and then hears the voice call out his name. He dashes into Eli's room and asks him what he wants. Again Eli tells him he didn't call out to him and tells him to go back to bed. It happens a third time, and at this point, Eli realizes God is speaking to Samuel. Eli utters these words to his young apprentice:

If the voice calls again, say, "Speak, God. I'm your servant, ready to listen."

1 Samuel 3:9, MSG

In the pages that follow, Samuel not only continues to hear from God, but he becomes the spokesperson for God to the nation of Israel. Along the way, God uses an old priest named Eli to guide and direct his young servant, soon-to-be leader. Eli makes his share of mistakes. He isn't always obedient. In fact, the entire second chapter of 1 Samuel talks about Eli's inability to lead his own family. But he is present for Samuel. He is in the right place at the right time to give Samuel the right nudge to listen to God speaking into his life.

1 Samuel tells us that "Samuel did not yet know the Lord: The word of the Lord had not yet been revealed to him." Isn't that the role we play now in the lives of these young people God has placed in our care? While they are with us, we get to teach and train them. We're going to help them know and understand the voice of God in their lives. And at some point, we are going to set them free, ready to listen and respond to the voice of the Lord on their own. Then it will be time for them to pass on what they learned to someone else.

Eli plays an important role in developing Samuel into a man of God. He is part of the process that shapes Samuel into the leader necessary for God's people at that time.

We are stewards of this same task. God has given us this opportunity as youth leaders, and we must approach it with humility and respect. Parents drop their kids off at church on a regular basis. Some of them do so with hopes that another significant adult will speak into the lives of their sons and daughters. They pray that God will bless their children. And some of them are bold enough to pray for God to develop their sons and daughters into leaders—people who will serve as godly influences in the lives of others.

My prayer is that you will be faithful in your role as an advisor, mentor, and spiritual guide, setting the example for those in your care. May your example be repeated in your students' examples, that others may follow their influence in the days ahead.

123
✳

bare
foot
MINISTRIES®

Helping youth workers guide students into spiritual formation for the mission of God.

———

Barefoot is devoted to providing churches around the world with practical, relevant, inspiring, and affordable resources to help youth and young adults find and follow Jesus.

Don't hesitate to contact us if we can help you or your faith community with our resources as you seek to guide students into spiritual formation for the mission of God!

———

www.BarefootMinistries.com

Other Books in the Youth Worker's Guide Series

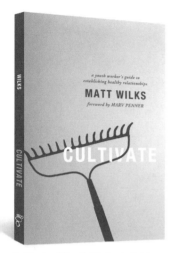

"Relationships are at the heart of whatever we do in youth ministry. Matt Wilks, writing out of his own personal and ministry journey, will help you rethink your relational world. He has done an admirable job of setting forth concrete suggestions that will ring true as you reflect on how you might better cultivate a healthier and more stable approach to your youth ministry."

— John H. Wilkinson, Ed. D
Executive Director, Toronto Youth For Christ

Cultivate: A Youth Worker's Guide to Establishing Healthy Relationships
By: Matt Wilks

"Finally, a book that addresses one of the most neglected and difficult seasons in a youth pastor's career. With rich personal experience, Tim walks the reader through practical ways to navigate those times of complex ministry transition."

— Jim Dekker, PhD,
co-director for the Center of Youth Ministries Studies,
associate professor of youth ministry,
North Park University and Seminary, Chicago, IL

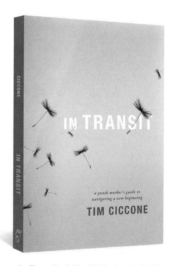

In Transit: A Youth Worker's Guide to Navigating a New Beginning
By: Tim Ciccone

Learn more at www.BarefootMinistries.com